95 Days in the NICU is a well-balanced tale of hope, perserverance, and belief.

95 DAYS *in the* NICU

Avie Banks

Edited by Allie Coker

ISBN: 978-1-9432582-0-8 (hard cover)
       978-1-7338973-4-1 (soft cover)

Library of Congress Control Number: 2016953441

Edited by: Allie Coker

Warren publishing

Published by Warren Publishing
Charlotte, NC
www.warrenpublishing.net
Printed in the United States

OUR STORY

ON DECEMBER 26TH, we were blessed to learn that after seven years of trying we were going to have a baby!

On January 12th, we confirmed that our little bundle of joy would be joining our family on August 13th.

Fast forward through three months of terrible morning sickness and discomfort that we forgot existed with the carrying and birth of our first child, Kenya, eleven years ago.

On April 4, we learned that we were having a little boy and all looked good. We also learned that with this pregnancy, a medication would be necessary to help prevent me from going into preterm labor.

That medication was scheduled to arrive on April 24th; however, God had another plan. On April 22nd, our water broke and we were in motion to welcome a new addition a lot earlier than planned.

After a week of constant monitoring by a great group of staff members at Harrisburg Hospital's Labor and Delivery and Antepartum units, we learned that our son was in distress and would need to be delivered by an emergency C-section.

On April 27th, at 2:30 p.m., we learned we were going to deliver him and by 4:42 p.m. we had a 1 lb 5.5 oz. little boy — *Clayton Davon Banks*.

This begins our story and you can pick up all the details of Clayton's journey on the following pages. We hope you enjoy as he tells you all about it!

~Bonswa, Avie, Kenya and Clayton

ACKNOWLEDGMENTS

THIS BOOK HAS TRULY BEEN a sincere labor of love for me. However, I would not be able to share these moments in our family's life with such optimism and grace had it not been for some great people, organizations and divine intervention that came full on to help us through it. Although I will venture to list some of those that touched our family I know I will inevitably miss some names that were just as significant to us. Please know that if you are not listed here your support, love, service and prayers did not go unnoticed and I and my family thank you.

I never got around to send formal thank you cards and I hope that this book and your name here lets you know that I and my family cannot thank you enough for all you did for us. From my family to you, we thank you and hope you too will forever be blessed as you were a blessing to us.

To our Dayspring Ministries church family, thank you for the meals, the prayers, the visits and the love. Thank you for supporting us through this difficult time and ensuring our first born continued to not skip a beat in all her activities during this time. We thank you for blessing us with baby supplies and the gift of love. You were a genuine demonstration of being one body and thy brother's keeper and not stopping the love and support once Clayton came home.

To the staff at Harrisburg Hospital (Pinnacle Health) NICU team—I cannot call out every name of the neonatologists, physician assistants, nurse practitioners, neurologists, ophthalmologists, surgeons, cardiologists, social workers and especially the nurses that loved my son as if he were their own. To his two primaries, Heather and Petra, words cannot thank you enough for crying with us and lifting us up when we couldn't understand all that was happening. Thank you for fighting for us and providing the most exceptional care possible. Each of you opened our eyes to the resources available to us, to the statistics and, with God, defied the odds that were stacked up against our micro preemie!

To the Central Penn March of Dimes, thank you for the resources in the NICU that helped me learn about what was ahead and for giving us a resource for connecting with other NICU families. Thank you for providing the kangaroo rocking chair that my daughter actively sought out when we arrived so that we all had comfort when cuddling with our son. Also, thank you for giving us a way to give back to the March of Dimes through the March for Babies event and encouraging us to raise awareness and funds for such a great cause!

To all our family and friends that fundraised, called, emailed, prayed and even visited; we appreciate everything you did, seen and unseen, and we appreciate your patience. For all those that read our daily blog and commented — a big thank you!

And, as with all things, I want to save my best thank you for last. This book in its entirety is dedicated to my daughter Kenya Michelle Banks, who was a pillar of support, strength and maturity throughout this journey. She will always be our first and proved why she is, and will forever be, so special to us. At eleven years old, your world was rocked with the birth of your brother. From the excitement of learning we were pregnant, to the fear of him coming early just like you, you didn't stop, and you kept going. You continued to be an honor student and you continued receiving awards, dancing, praising and standing. From the moment I went to the hospital to the day your brother came home, you loved him, you held him, you worried for him and you prayed for him. Just as we taught you, you often reassured us and you provided great crafts and a lot of fun for the NICU staff. You were an angel and to my angel, I dedicate this book because without your strength and without knowing what we experienced in having you who knows where we would be! Thank you to our first love for our first heartbeat, for our first survivor and for even helping me with writing this book. Our preemies are our life and you and your brother continue to make life worth living!

PROLOGUE

A S A LITTLE GIRL, I was the one who had my whole life planned out, and, as corny as it sounds, I wanted the large ranch home with the wrap-around porch sporting white rocking chairs, two kids and a dog all nestled into a yard enclosed with a white picket fence. It was my dream and it was going to be super easy to achieve as I was a smart girl going to one of the top universities in North Carolina (Go Heels!) I was going to have a partner one day in life and love to make all these dreams come true.

But, God had another plan. He mixed portions of my original plan with life interventions to teach me lessons and show me how to make choices which sent me down a different path.

I did meet the man of my dreams in college and we had our beautiful daughter soon thereafter, quickly learning that there was a big difference from having a baby at 33 weeks versus 40 weeks at full term. But, that wasn't where our 95 day journey began, that came later. With our precious daughter, we spent just 10 days in the NICU and she only had mild issues during her stay — namely jaundice. No surgeries, no multiple doctors, no issues with feeding, just the lights. Although she was only 3 lbs 13 oz at birth she quickly got up to 5 lbs and began eating with no difficulties. She was quickly able to come home.

Of course, that is not where the story ends, as that is only two of the dreams fulfilled (great husband, wonderful daughter); I still had a few more to check off the list. So, two years later we got our ranch house with a full length porch (but no picket fence) and were well on our way! Both my husband and I were doing well in our careers and it was about time for our daughter to head to school when the itch for a second child came.

We tried for about two years to have another child but with no success we decided that we were okay with one. But, two years later we got that itch again and we really wanted to have another child as our oldest was growing so quickly. We tried for about a year even seeing a fertility specialist and moving on to try hormone injections and IUF, all with no success. By 2010 we took that news to mean that we would raise one great daughter and be completely content with God's plan for us.

However, in June 2011 we relocated from North Carolina to Pennsylvania for work. In October, we felt that it would be great to add that dog to the family and Felipe became the best adoption ever. By December 2011, I found myself really ill. I had recently returned home from an international trip and thought I had food poisoning. My mom quickly informed me otherwise and insisted I should check to ensure nothing else was wrong. The day after Christmas my husband and I ventured out to catch some deals and thought — why not — let's pick up a test for the fun of it! We got home and the shock, the excitement, the *oh no, is this for real?* happened and yes... we were pregnant! We were actually pregnant.

I had terrible morning sickness. I visited my doctors routinely and was part of my health insurance high risk pregnancy program. And still... I hope you enjoy reading about the next steps of our journey that taught us what to expect when you are expecting a micro preemie!

Day 1
It's My Birthday

Today, I entered the world with a long road ahead. No one said the road would be easy but our steps are ordered by the Lord! Continue to check in to see how I grow.

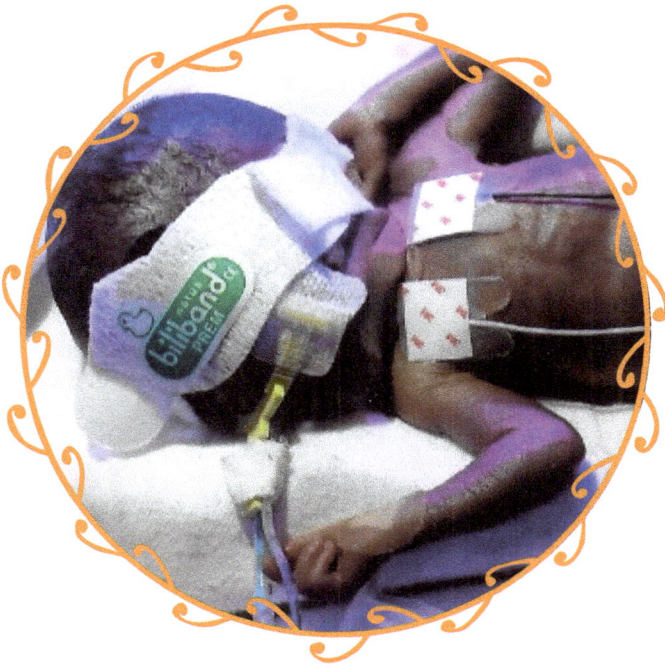

DAY 2
ALL HOOKED UP   *April 28, 2012*

Today, I am all hooked up. My vent is on to help me breathe and I have a few lines in my umbilical cord to help me get my nutrients. My lungs are still growing and I can't drink milk just yet, so these things are helping me until I get stronger.

I am so tiny, my dad's wedding ring fits around my arm with room to spare!

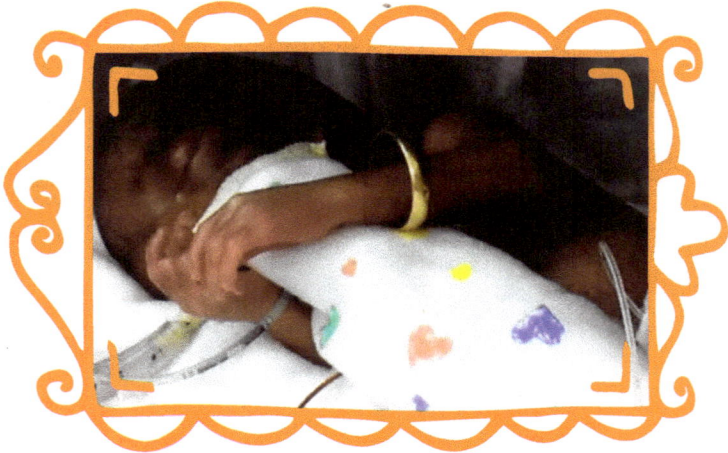

DAY 3
LET THERE BE LIGHT

April 29, 2012

Since some of my labs are a little out of whack, they have me under blue lights to help with my liver function. I have some great shades for my eyes to protect them from the lights but my skin gets a little dry.

But, as in the days of creation; God said "Let there be light; and there was light." God saw the light and it was good.

So, until my blood levels stabilize; let the light so shine on me.

Today the doctors did a scan on my head and found that I had a lot of bleeding *but*, it is okay for now and they are going to continue to monitor my head size and the bleeding.

The doctors also did a scan on my heart. I have a hole that has not closed and the doctors are going to monitor it to see if it will close on its own or get smaller. If not, they may have to do surgery.

But, with every test comes a new testimony... keep checking in to see how I do!

Good news though... my mom was strong enough to go home today!

DAY 5
MORE BLOOD PLEASE

May 1, 2012

    Another day with more tests. My blood levels are a little low so I have received a few blood and platelet transfusions. This is expected for a little guy like me. The nurses are trying to get mom and dad to change my diaper even though they feel I am too small but any day now I know they will try.

DAY 6
DAD'S TOUCH

May 2, 2012

Today everything is the same. Dad came to visit as he does every day but this day was different because he took my temperature today. It was our first touch and it was great! I look forward to feeling mom and my sister.

My sister, Kenya, hasn't been able to visit because she has dance practice. The nurse and dad helped me make a card to let her know that I miss her and look forward to seeing her tomorrow. I even took a picture and put it on the card.

Today was another day of firsts for me. Today Grandma finally got to see my eyes! Even better, my mommy held me today. Well, sort of. Each night the nurses weigh me and have to lift me off my bed. Tonight mommy lifted me and held me for my weight. Of course my weight was good but it felt even better to have mom hold me.

Plus, Kenya was back to see me so I had lots of visitors and was a little tired by the end of the visit.

LOVE

Each day I am getting stronger. All of my labs are going in the right direction. Grandma went home today after being here with me every day. Mom, Dad and Kenya still come see me each morning and night. Today, Kenya took my temperature under my arm and I think I am stronger because I wiggled all over the place. But she took my temperature anyway no matter how much I wiggled. Dad did my weight and held me this time. Oh, and yesterday I got my first bath with sterile water as that is all my fragile skin can handle.

Oh, and today, I am a week old.

DAY 9
CINCO DE MAYO

May 5, 2012

Today my family brought a basket of candy to share with the staff to celebrate Cinco de Mayo. I was pretty quiet today. Everyone is excited because I am scheduled to have heart surgery on Tuesday to close the hole. Today my mom changed my diaper... yay. Kenya took my temperature again and Dad helped with my weight.

The nurses are measuring my head size daily due to the bleeding and my size is staying consistent around 22 and 21.5 cm.

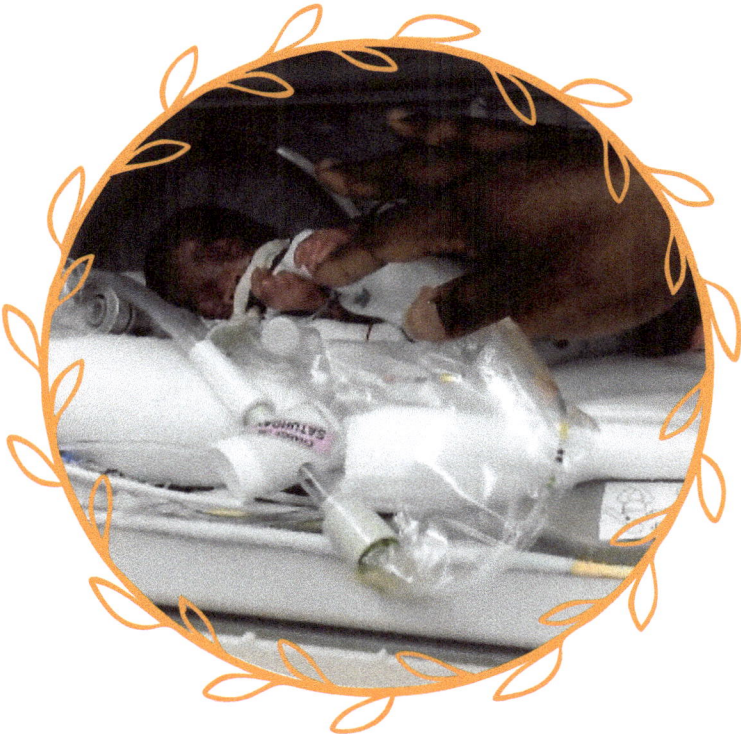

DAY 10
SMALL CHANGES

I had a good day and a good night. I am still on room air on my vent so we look forward to getting rid of this machine after the surgery. My mom keeps calling me a wiggle worm because I keep moving off of my gel heated bedding. Kenya took my temperature today and I was a little cold so they turned up the heat in my personal sauna.

My bilirubin went up so it looks like the blue light isn't going anywhere anytime soon. Everything else is the same but I have gained half an ounce so now I weigh 1 lb 6 oz.

Day 11
ANTICIPATION

May 7, 2012

Today I had a scan of my head and my heart done and all is still as expected so I have surgery tomorrow morning to close the hole in my heart. With my surgery, I can get off my vent and they will remove my lines in my umbilical cord and my mom and dad will finally get to hold me!

Isaiah 53:5
"But he was pierced for our transgressions, he was crushed for our iniquities; the punishment that brought us peace was on him, and by his wounds we are healed."

I had my surgery today to close the hole in my heart and it went swimmingly. The surgeon said I did a very good job! I looked up and saw Mom and Dad before the surgery and then was too tired after the surgery to even move. When Mom and Dad came back tonight I wiggled a little when I heard them and then the nurse gave me more meds so I was back fast asleep.

The team tried to put my PICC line in (like an IV line where they can give me fluids, medication, blood or nutrients) today but they couldn't get it in, so they are going to try again tomorrow. My doctor also said that they are going to take me off the ventilator tomorrow morning and I will be transitioning to a CPAP machine that they will take on and off every couple of hours. Oh, and I get to try to drink some of my mom's milk again and I hear she has a lot stored up for me.

DAY 13
MUCH PRAYER, MUCH POWER (FREEDOM)   *May 9, 2012*

Boy, today was a busy day! First, I didn't get to disconnect from my ventilator today; my oxygen levels aren't quite where they are supposed to be. The doctor says in the next couple of days hopefully I will be ready.

The good news? No more lines in my umbilical cord. The PICC line went in — Mom and the nurse prayed today that it would be successful and it was. But even better news, I was able to get out of my Isolete (my enclosed bed) today *and* my dad got to hold me. They wrapped me up like a burrito so I would stay warm and then put me right in my dad's arms. We looked into each other's eyes and it was great.

Tomorrow, Mom and I will do what they call kangaroo care. This is when Mom gets to hold me skin to skin for an hour. It will be great and they are going to try to reintroduce feeding to me again tomorrow. The first time I tried to eat, my stomach wasn't ready and I couldn't digest it; but I am thinking positive thoughts that tomorrow will be successful.

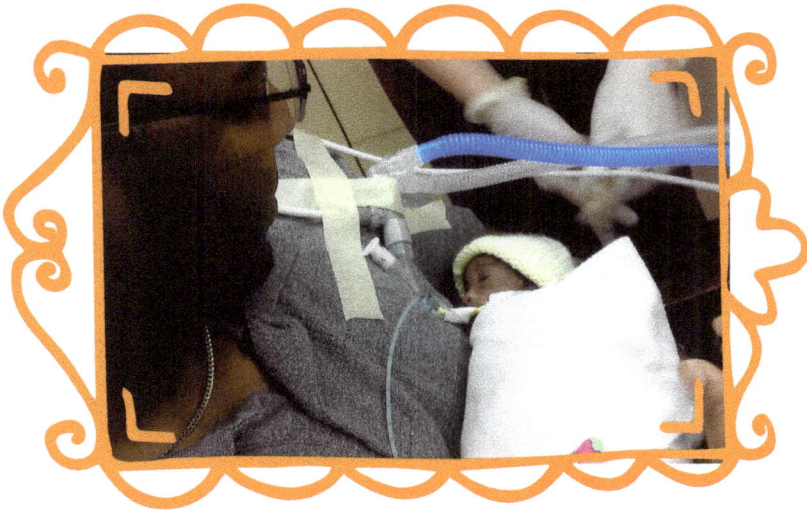

Well, no one said the road would be easy. That is what my mom told the nurse today. We weren't able to do kangaroo care today because my PICC line location began to swell. The nurse had to remove it and they tried to put in a new one. It didn't work so the surgeon had to come in and insert the line late this evening.

So, maybe tomorrow we can do kangaroo care. But, I am off of the blue lights and weighed in yesterday at 1 lb 7 oz. Oh, and I got to have some of my mom's milk today. If I digest it well tonight, I will begin feedings every 6 hours... yay!

Isaiah 40:31
"But they that wait upon the Lord shall renew their strength; they shall mount up with wings as eagles; they shall run, and not be weary; and they shall walk, and not faint."

DAY 15
A HOPPING GOOD TIME

May 11, 2012

Yes, I know your question and the answer is... I got to do kangaroo care (K-care) with Mom! It was great. Before we started I was just so excited I couldn't be still in my bed, but as soon as they placed me on Mom's chest I settled right down. I look forward to K-care every day. Mom even bought me a new blanket to use during K-care today with one of the gift cards that was so graciously provided to us. We had to borrow one this morning but now we have our very own special blanket to keep just for K-care.

I also got a new bed today; they change my bed every week so that they can clean them. But even better, my stomach likes Mom's milk now so I am finally having feedings every 6 hours. The doctor is sure that I am getting off the vent soon because I am doing so well. I winked at Kenya tonight and opened my eyes really wide when I heard Dad's voice. Today was a good day.

Thank God It's Friday (TGIF)... I am now two weeks old!

Today my ventilator was taken off! I had a few moments of freedom and my dad took a picture of my face free of equipment. The nurses that have been with me previously and even the doctors came over to celebrate me moving from my ventilator to the SiPAP. The SiPAP is almost like a CPAP machine but the air goes into the nose at a different rate where the CPAP has a continuous flow of air going. I did very well all day on the SiPAP so hopefully no more ventilator.

It was very weird not having the tubes down my throat so I moved my tongue a lot when they first took the ventilator off and didn't realize that I could finally close my mouth all the way. I blew lots of bubbles for a while because my mouth was full of saliva.

My feeding is now every four hours instead of every six since I am tolerating the feedings so well. Kenya took my temperature, Mom changed my diaper and Dad did K-care with me today and I did beautifully. We even got to use my new blanket. When the nurse put me back into my bed, I tried to wiggle right off because it wasn't as comfortable as Dad's chest.

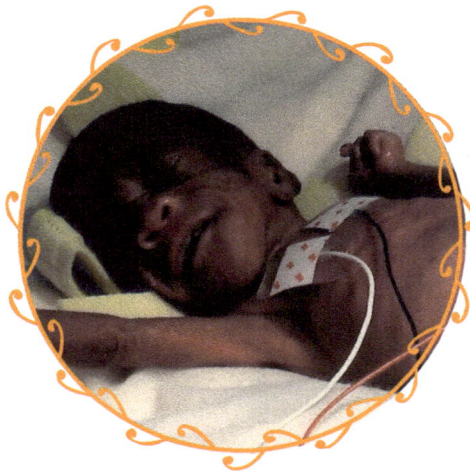

DAY 17
HAPPY MOTHER'S DAY   *May 13, 2012*

Happy Mother's Day! Today was just another day of staying steady. The doctors have increased my feedings from 1 mL to 2 mL every 3 hours and then they will increase it by 1 mL every 12 hours.

Today, I did K-care with Mom and didn't alarm on my machines one time which is great. Kenya took my temperature again and Mom changed my diaper. Dad took his daily batch of pictures as well.

The nurses helped me to make a special Mother's Day card with my footprints in the shape of a heart and my handprints as well. Tomorrow I have another scan of my head to see how the bleeding is doing. I am praying for a good report.

Boy, breathing on my own is a lot of work. I may have to go back on my ventilator because I sometimes forget that I have to breathe on my own continuously now. The nurses, Dad or Mom have to pat me on my butt or rub my back or tummy a few times to remind me to breathe and to get the machines to stop alarming because I sometimes take too long of a rest.

Also, since I am using so much energy I am losing a little weight. I was down to 1 lb 4 oz but am now a little above my birth weight at 1 lb 6 oz. They are still increasing my feedings and I love them! I am now at 4 mL every three hours with a 1 mL increase every 12 hours. I also get a bit of caffeine (2 mL) every 24 hours as the doctors say this will help me with my breathing and lung development. My mom and dad just think it makes me more of a wiggle worm.

I got to do K-care again today with Mom, but I alarmed a lot because of my breaks in breathing. I also had the hiccups and Kenya and Mom had the giggles because my voice with each hiccup sounded like a little mouse. Mom, Dad and Kenya got to hear me for the first time tonight. Dad took my temperature and changed my diaper for the first time.

Oh, and the scan of my head showed that the bleeding on the right side is still the same (grade 4) but the bleeding on the left side has gotten a little worse (grade 3). They will do another scan next Monday, but because I am so small no intervention is planned for now; they will just continue to monitor it.

It was a busy day and I worked hard, but I have a lot of work ahead so I will keep pushing forward.

Philippians 3:14
"I press toward the mark for the prize of the high calling of God in Christ Jesus."

Today was a better day. I remembered to breathe more often today which meant less alarms and happier nurses and family members. The doctor said that for me to alarm is normal so they are going to continue the SiPAP for now and aren't planning to switch me back to the ventilator.

My labs are continuing to get better, my creatinine and BUN levels (which looks at my kidney function) are finally getting better as well as my total bilirubin (which looks at my liver function) so that was exciting. My platelets jumped up which made the doctors very happy and my white blood count are getting better. My hemoglobin and hematocrit levels are still not where the doctors want them to be so I received some more blood today.

I am up to 6 mL of milk every three hours so still doing well with feedings which means they are lowering the amount of lipids they are giving me. Mom brings me fresh milk each morning. My last round of antibiotics end on May 23rd so hopefully soon after the antibiotics end, they will remove the PICC line which is how my lipids and antibiotics are delivered.

I got a full bath today and it completely relaxed me for when Mom, Dad and Kenya came to visit this afternoon.

Day 20
Thank You

Everyone has been so nice to me in the hospital and encourages me to continue to do my best and to try hard. Today, I was able to use a pacifier for the first time. I enjoyed it and was able to breathe through my nose and suck on my pacifier at the same time this morning.

I am gaining a little weight and am now 12 and ³/₄ inches so I have grown just a little. They are starting to fortify my milk with some extra calories (about 22) to help me start to gain some weight. Dad did K-care with me today. No other changes so everything was good.

The rest of this post is to thank you for your many prayers and encouraging words on my guestbook page and the tributes in my honor. Mom, Dad and Kenya continue to tell me how many people have provided meals, cards, gift cards and tons of love and support since I have been born. Thank you for taking this journey with me and most of all continuing to pray for me and my family as we continue on this journey! I look forward to going home and having the opportunity to meet each of you. Mom and Dad are going to print out my pictures, journal and guestbook to put in an album for me to look back over my early days of life to see how truly blessed I have been and will continue to be.

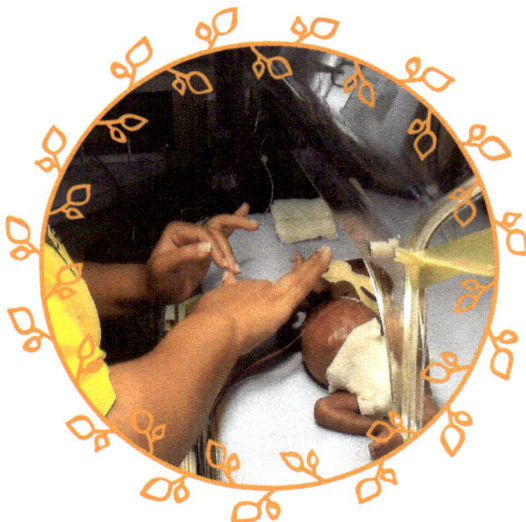

Today I was fussy; so fussy you could actually hear my soft cries. No tears came down but my face said it all. Mom, Dad and Kenya were so excited to hear my little voice that they just laughed as I tried to cry. Since my cries only made them smile, I stopped and went on to let Kenya take my temperature and Mom change my diaper. Mom did rub the pacifier over my lips so I sucked it for a little while and that too helped me to relax.

I am tolerating the fortified milk and weighed 1 lb 6.4 oz. I did K-care with Mom today. Everything else was just another day.

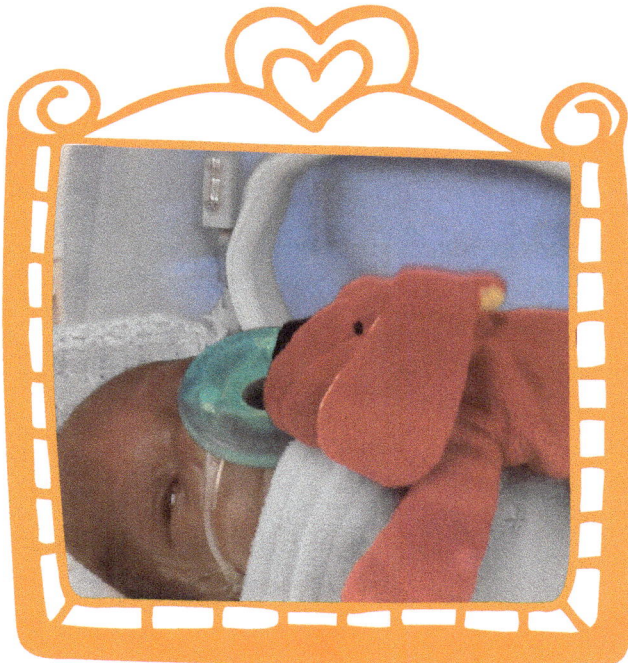

Nothing but smooth sailing today. I did give my nurses a run for their money with a few alarms but I just wanted to be sure they were on their toes.

Today, the doctors told me that my renal function (kidneys) is now where they should be and my liver function (bilirubin levels) is still being monitored. They may add another medication to help bring down these levels. The only other areas currently being monitored are my respiratory function and the bleeding in my head (intraventricular hemorrhage). I have been able to go to room air on my SiPAP but when I alarm they have to move me up a little for additional air support. In addition, they are, of course, still monitoring the bleeding in my head. The good news is that the bleeding in my head is treatable if it doesn't resolve itself. So everything is still smooth sailing.

I am three weeks old today... yay! Kenya took my temperature and helped the nurse change the linen in my bed. Mom changed my diaper and Dad did K-care with me tonight. *I love my family*! Today I weighed 1 lb 6.6 oz.

DAY 23
THE GOOD, THE BAD AND THE FUNNY   *May 19, 2012*

The Good
This evening I was breathing very well and my face is free again. My dad is very happy having the SiPAP off because my head can go back to a normal shape. Kenya took my temperature, Mom changed my diaper, and Dad took more pictures.

The Bad
I am off of my SiPAP because I had to go back on my ventilator. I was really tired a lot today and kept setting off alarms so the doctor decided to put me back on my ventilator. By the evening, I was letting the machine do all the work because I was so tired so no K-care for me tonight.

The Funny
I am starting to move and grab onto everything around me. Today, my hand found its way down my diaper.

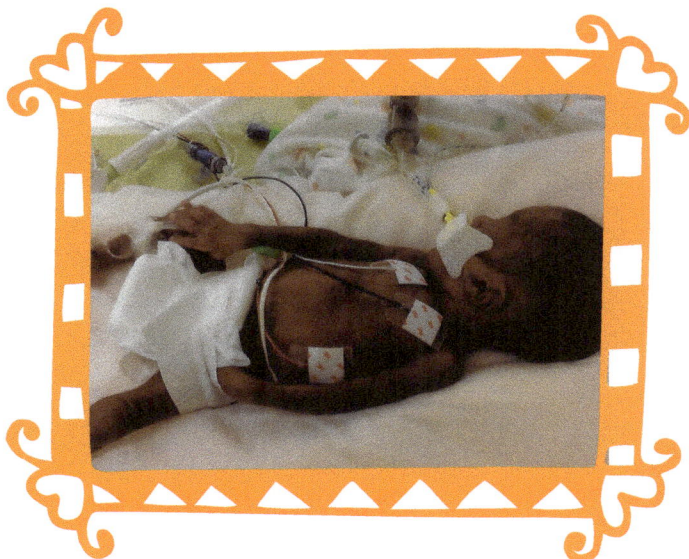

The plan is that I get my PICC line out on Wednesday which means one less line on my body. The doctor came to look at my head yesterday evening and said that they are going to continue to monitor the bleeding and he hopes to see my head grow which means that the brain is developing as normal. Today my head size was 22.5 cm; which is a little bit of growth. I have another head scan tomorrow.

I have a little irritation on my tummy so they have started a new topical ointment to help clear it up. Today, I weighed 1 lb 6.8 oz. I continued to let my vent do the majority of the work today but I did actually do a few breaths while Mom, Dad and Kenya visited today. The nurses said I was a good boy today. So, the plan is to continue to keep improving and taking it one day at a time.

Jeremiah 29:11 (NIV84)
"For I know the plans I have for you," declares the LORD, "plans to prosper you and not to harm you, plans to give you hope and a future."

Today I had my head scan to check on the status of the bleeding. We didn't get the results from the doctors. If anything was wrong they usually call my mom and dad or pull them to the side as soon as they arrive to visit me, so we trust that no news is good news.

I was really quiet today; a little wiggly when Kenya took my temperature. I missed seeing Dad today, but he has a stomach virus so he stayed home so he did not get me or anyone else sick. I did K-care with Mom and my SPO2 levels (monitors the oxygen transport in my body) were at 99-100% almost the entire time I lay on Mom. I didn't alarm and took a lot of breaths on my own. My ventilator was able to stay at room air (a few times it was just above at 22; room air is at 21) which is also progress. I am getting stronger every day.

The irritation on my stomach is starting to look better and clear up a little too.

I am growing more. Today I weighed 1 lb 8 oz. The doctors have also increased my feedings to 10 mL (up from 9 mL) every three hours. In addition, I am now getting vitamins, iron and sodium as part of my diet to help with my growth and development.

Remember I told you they were monitoring my liver function? Well, my bilirubin level (which measures my liver function) went down from 3.1 to 2.3 which is great as they just need it to get below two. They started me on some medicine last week to help with this and they are going to keep me on it until my levels go below two. The next check will be next Tuesday.

The results of my head scan did not show any change so they are going to just continue to monitor it. Kenya checked my temperature as usual and Mom did K-care with me and Dad was able to see me today because he felt better.

DAY 27
I LIKE TO MOVE IT
May 23, 2012

Today I was the biggest wiggle worm of all. I honestly thought that I could crawl today. I turned myself off of my side onto my back because I was wiggling so much. I moved and moved all morning during Mom's visit and again all evening when Mom and Dad visited.

I weighed in at 1lb 8.6 oz today and was 32 cm. Today was also bath day and I didn't like it one bit. I tried to jump and crawl away from the nurse with all my little strength but nothing worked to get away. I also had my PICC line removed as planned so it was great to have my leg free again.

My umbilical cord stump finally came off last night so I have a nice, clean stomach. No new updates otherwise, just being my little wiggly self and looking around more at my nurse, Mom and Dad.

DAY 28
SLOW AND EASY

May 24, 2012

Today was a slow and uneventful day. There were no changes for me today. My head size was 23 cm and I weighed in at 1 lb 8.6 oz. I am up to 13 mL every three hours with 28 additional calories being given to continue to help me grow.

Kenya took my temperature today and Dad changed my diaper. Mom did K-care with me tonight and I got to use a new blanket that members of our church gave me, so things were good. It was a slow day but an easy one so I am happy. Sometimes uneventful days can be the best days.

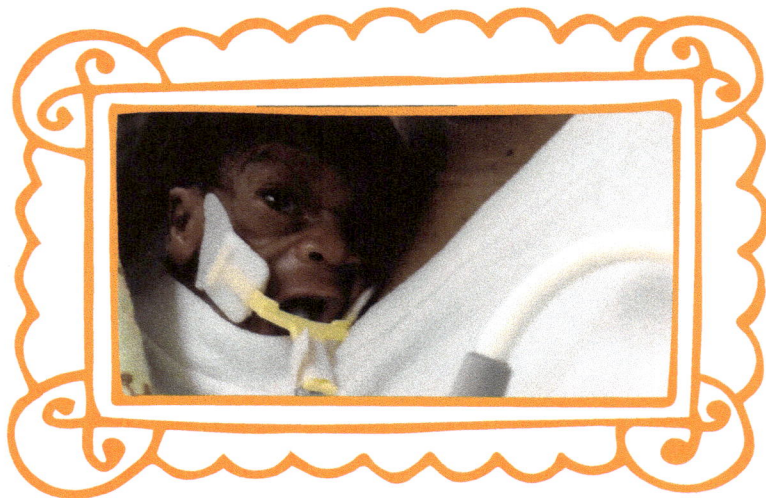

DAY 29
MY HAPPY PLACE

May 25, 2012

I am four weeks old! I was in my happy place a lot today. Kenya took my temperature and Mom changed my diaper. But my happy place is lying on my belly with my arms and knees tucked just a little underneath me. The only place happier than that is K-care time. Today I did K-care with Mom for an extended time because I was such a good boy.

My bilirubin levels are finally stable so the doctors took me off another medication today. My blood levels were a little too low so I had to get some blood. Otherwise, it was a great day to relax and take in my family. I had my eyes open a lot so Dad took tons of pictures.

Day 30
All Quiet on the Northern Front

May 26, 2012

It was just a normal Saturday for me. Everyone is still just watching to see how much I grow. As I grow I get more food and calorie supplements that will help me keep packing on the pounds.

Mom, Dad and Kenya came to see me today and I was really good for them. I loved stretching my legs though which caused me to get a little wiggly so sometimes Mom and Kenya had to hold their hands in front of my feet so they would stay tucked. When they did this I settled right down and would go back to sleep.

So, today was a quiet day for me here in Pennsylvania!

When the doctors told my mom that they were going to have to do an emergency C-section they also told her that with me only being 24 weeks in the gestational period, I was just at the "viable" stage meaning that there was a 50/50 chance I would survive. The first 24-72 hours were critical.

Well, here I am; born on 4/27/2012 at 1 lb 5.5 oz and today I am officially one month old weighing 1 lb 10.8 oz. God is so good! He allowed the doctors, nurses and all the staff to be used by Him so that He could work through them to perform His good and perfect Will.

Today was another great day; I finally got to do K-care with Dad (which he calls Clayton-care and K-care now stands for Kenya-care because we can't leave her out!) Mom changed my diaper and Kenya took my temperature. I was such a big boy that I just looked around a lot again today seeing all who was around, knowing that each person continues to play a key part in God's plan for my life and he leaves nothing up to chance!

Revelation 21:6
He said to me: "It is done. I am the Alpha and the Omega, the Beginning and the End. To the thirsty I will give water without cost from the spring of the water of life."

Happy Memorial Day! I have big news. Today the doctors and nurses decided to take me off of the ventilator again. I was doing so well on my ventilator that they have now moved me back to the SiPAP. By the evening when Mom, Dad and Kenya came to visit I was doing really well breathing on my own. Since I had such a big transition today, we didn't do Clay-care to allow me time to adjust and not use too much energy on anything other than breathing.

The doctors also increased my feedings to 14 mL every 3 hours. My weight increased again to 1 lb 11.8 oz. My head size is 23.5 cm. My head scan was moved from today to tomorrow so we will get an update on the bleeding in my head then. The doctors say that my head is growing at an expected rate.

My family brought in treats for the NICU staff today to help them celebrate Memorial Day. Although, I couldn't enjoy all the festivities going on outside, I had a *happy* Memorial Day and I hope you did too!

Today I had my head ultrasound and it showed no changes. The doctors said that this is good news so we are pleased that things are status quo at the moment with my head.

I am on my second day back on the SiPAP and I actually gained weight again today. I weighed 1 lb 12.2 oz. Yesterday, Dad took another picture with his wedding ring on me and it wouldn't go over my fist so I have definitely grown! This evening the nurse got me all ready (temperature, diaper change and weight) before my family came to visit but Mom did an extra-long Clay-care with me today when they arrived. I had the hiccups again which made Mom, Dad and Kenya laugh but they all got to hear me sneeze for the first time. Since they liked it so much I sneezed twice just for them.

Today was another good day of moving in the right direction.

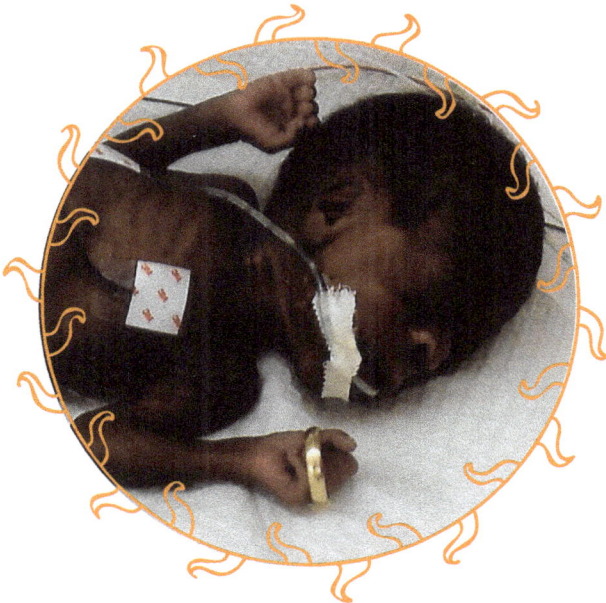

Day 34
First Kiss

May 30, 2012

Today was another good day. I started the day with my pacifier in my mouth. When I was on the ventilator I wasn't able to have my pacifier. I did a great job breathing and keeping my pacifier in my mouth.

Today I weighed 1 lb 12.8 oz. Mom gave me a bath for the first time today and the nurse washed my hair. Dad held my hand and talked to me while I was waiting for my bed to be made. Before I went back to bed Mom and Dad gave me my first kiss. I was wide awake and looked at them both with great excitement. It was so great to get my first kiss from Mom and Dad.

The doctors said everything looks good so my feedings were increased to 15 mL (equals 0.5 oz of Mom's milk) every three hours.

After my bath, I was very relaxed and looked at Mom and Dad for a long time before I drifted off to sleep for the night.

May 31, 2012

I had my first relocation experience today. I got moved to a new area in the NICU. The NICU has about 8 different pods (areas) where they keep about six to eight preemies in each pod. I was in the same pod since I was born but have watched a number of my friends move across the aisle into another pod as they grew stronger. Today was my turn! They moved me over with some of my friends! My mom, dad, Kenya and nurses were very excited for me to make the move.

I did Clay-care with Mom today and she even got me out of my bed all by herself. Kenya took my temperature and Dad took a few pictures. Today I was about 1 lb 15 oz which is a big jump so the nurse said that she was going to re-check it just to make sure it was accurate, but I will enjoy the extra few ounces until then!

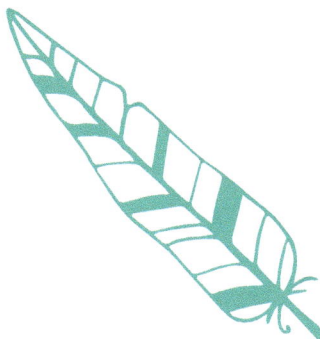

The NICU has been really busy the past few days with new arrivals but for a little guy like me that isn't requiring much attention, it was a day of tranquility. Mom and Dad came to visit and Dad did Clayton-care with me this evening.

The doctors increased my feedings to 17 mL every 3 hours and are thinking of moving me to using a nasal tube across my nose to give me extra oxygen. This will allow me to take off my SiPAP head gear for a few hours to give my nose, ears and head a little rest from being strapped.

My weight decreased to 1 lb 13.6 oz today but we expected that since I had a large increase yesterday. I am still hoping and have faith that I will reach 2 lbs by the end of this weekend!

Hebrews 11:1
"Now faith is the substance of things hoped for, the evidence of things not seen."

DAY 37
TEMPORARY RELIEF
June 2, 2012

Yesterday marked five weeks for me. Each day provides a new opportunity for strength and growth. Today, the doctors were true to their word and started weaning me off of the SiPAP. I have now moved to having a break from the SiPAP for four hours out of the day. Now, a nasal cannula is placed under my nose to provide a constant stream of oxygen support for two hours in the morning and two hours in the evening. Both of these periods are during the time Mom, Dad and Kenya come to visit. With the new oxygen support, I get to have my head and nose free of the head gear and I am doing more of the work to breathe. I was so impressed with the new oxygen support that I began breathing very well on my own.

I weighed 1 lb 14 oz so I grew a little from yesterday. Kenya took my temperature after catching up on some much needed rest after our church's youth lock-in. Mom and Dad both had a chance to change my diaper. Mom did Clayton-care this morning and Dad brought Uncle Kris C to visit with me today and did Clayton-care this evening. I actually got to come out and play twice today for a total of two hours!

Today was another great day full of next steps and seeing new faces!

Today, I weighed 1 lb 15 oz — just 1 oz away from 2 lbs. Dad gave me a bath today, Kenya took my temperature and Mom held me during a modified Clay-care (it wasn't skin to skin; I was wrapped up like a burrito this time).

Today, I want to share my vision and I am going to step out on faith like Peter did on the boat when he was facing a mighty storm. As I go through the challenges of being premature and while the doctors continue to monitor my lungs, weight and head some may choose to focus on the challenges that I currently have and *could* have in the future, but I choose to trust God and focus on my future while enjoying the present.

MY VISION
I have a vision of going home, without extra support, with Mom and Dad very soon and meeting all of the people that have prayed for my continued growth. I have a vision of running and jumping at the playground and going to a normal daycare with other children that didn't have the same challenges as me. I have a vision of Dad making me breakfast and Mom packing my lunch for my first day of school. I envision playing football, basketball, soccer or baseball with other little boys one day. I have a vision of camping out with Kenya when I can't get to sleep. I have a vision of sharing my testimony with others to show just what a good God we serve.

Habakkuk 2:2-3 (KJV)

"And the Lord answered me, and said, Write the vision, and make it plain upon tables, that he may run that readeth it. For the vision is yet for an appointed time, but at the end it shall speak, and not lie: though it tarry, wait for it; because it will surely come, it will not tarry."

I didn't quite get to 2 lbs. I weighed 1 lb 15.6 oz. So close to my goal. Today the doctors increased my time on the nasal cannula to three hours and then six hours on the SiPAP throughout the day. I will alternate between the two.

I did Clay-care with Mom, Dad changed my diaper and Kenya took my temperature. I made a lot of cooing noises this evening trying to talk to everyone. It was really fun to actually start to communicate with my voice and not just with my eyes and wiggling my arms and legs.

Until tomorrow, I will keep eating and sleeping. I'm saving my voice and energy to celebrate as soon as I hit 2 lbs.

Today was full of surprises. Kenya held me today for the first time (see the picture in photos) and she held me for a whole hour! I did so well because it was great being in her arms.

The doctors have now moved me off of the SiPAP and I am on the C-PAP machine now getting continuous air because I was doing so well on the SiPAP and nasal cannula. The goal is to get me using the nasal cannula only. I had my head ultrasound yesterday, and this morning the doctors said there was no change which is good. Oh, and the best news of all — it only took me 40 days and 40 nights but today was the day; I am weighing in at 2 lbs 1 oz.

Mom went out of town tonight so she stayed extra-long visiting with me this morning Dad changed my diaper today and is becoming a pro at it. Kenya also took my temperature. It was another day of great improvement, new experiences and celebration.

Today was another good day. Dad visited me twice today since Mom was still out of town during doctor's rounds this morning. Mom surprised me with a late night visit when she got back into town, but I was worn out from having such a good time with Dad and Kenya.

Tonight, Kenya took my temperature and Dad changed my diaper, then Kenya held me again and I did well.

I didn't do much tonight because I was really tired. There were no major updates today, so I was able to rest well all throughout the day knowing God has me in the palm of his hand.

LOVE

I am making good progress with my breathing. I am now on the nasal cannula for six hours and on the C-PAP for 6 hours. I was able to go to room air (volume of 21) already on both. The doctors have been really impressed with how well I am doing.

Kenya took my temperature tonight, Dad changed my diaper and Mom held me. Dad had to give me my pacifier tonight to soothe me. Since I found my voice, I am starting to tell you exactly how I feel and get a little vocal when I get fussy. I am still growing and actually could fit into the outfit the nurses dressed me in today!

With all of this progress, I am moving closer and closer to going home.

Day 43
Overstimulated

Do you know why I hiccup sometimes? I didn't know either until today. When Mom, Dad and Kenya came to visit me today the nurse had finished most of my care activities (temperature and diaper change). Tonight was bath night. Instead of Clay-care, Dad gave me a bath and washed my hair. It was a nice, *long*, warm bath. When Dad finished washing my head and started to dry me off, I got the hiccups. The nurse stated that when babies are overstimulated they can sometimes get the hiccups. Since Dad gave me such a thorough washing and rubbed lotion all over me I was very stimulated.

After it was all done, Kenya helped the nurse change out my bedding and Mom held me while they got the bed all setup. To keep me from getting cold, Mom wrapped me in a snuggly fleece blanket. I was wide awake during all of these activities and didn't put up much of a fuss tonight.

Today, I am six weeks old and weigh 2 lbs 2 oz.

I had a good day today. Guess what, Dad didn't change my diaper today; Mom did. Kenya took my temperature and Dad did Clay-care with me for over an hour. I loved it and was in a deep sleep the entire time. Dad even fell asleep too.

I weigh 2 lbs 2.7 oz and the doctors have increased my time on the nasal cannula to nine hours, then I go back on the C-PAP for three hours and continue on this cycle throughout the day.

Some friends generously gave me a lot of clothes to wear and additional items for Mom and Dad to begin getting the house ready when I come home. I can be in the hospital up until Mom's original due date of August 13th but the nurses think that I should be coming home before then so it is never too soon to get ready for my arrival home.

2 Corinthians 9:10

"For God is the one who provides seed for the farmer and then bread to eat. In the same way, he will provide and increase your resources and then produce a great harvest of generosity in you."

My mom and dad are still working through the differences of having a little boy vs. having a little girl. It has been so long since Mom and Dad had to change diapers for a little boy that they forgot the most important rule — *don't leave the hose uncovered*! First it was Dad; except every time he would change me I would have a bowel movement immediately following. With Mom she just can't remember to quickly cover me with the new diaper and I get her every time. Today, it was a waterfall and I just missed her shirt but did manage to mess up my bedding and clothes. The nurse was not too happy with Mom as she had to change everything out. I was already a little stinky from when Dad changed me so tonight was another bath night.

Both Mom and Dad did my diaper tonight and Kenya held me again before she had to leave for dance practice — she has a big show this weekend!

I am still growing. The doctors have increased my feeds to 18 mL every three hours and my nurse said tomorrow it is bye-bye C-PAP and hello nasal cannula full-time. Now that I have finally gotten the hang of breathing on my own, hopefully Mom will get the hang of wrapping up "The Hose."

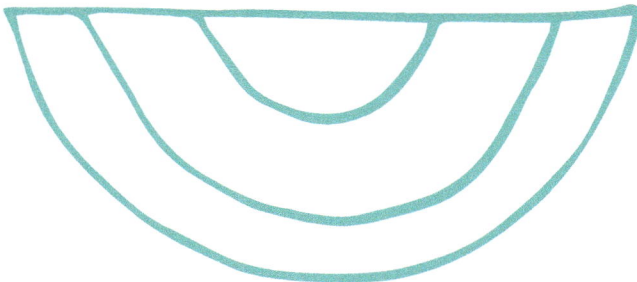

Each Monday morning, usually between midnight and 3 am, the team comes in and does an ultrasound to check on the effects of the bleeding in my head. The results of today's ultrasound showed some change. My left side (which was a grade 3) shows that the ventricles are getting smaller which is great; however, the right side (which was a grade 4) now shows some scarring on my brain.

As my brain was developing on the right side there was so much bleeding that scar tissue developed in one area. If you look at me today, you wouldn't even know that my little head had so much going on inside. The doctors and nurses were great and told my mom and dad of all the risks that could result from the scar tissue. Because I am little and my brain is still growing the scar tissue could cause minor long-term damage. Alternatively, I could develop cerebral palsy (which affects the brain and nervous system controlling my fine motor skills). Because I am a preemie when I get to go home (which is still a couple months away), I will have a team working with me that will include my pediatrician, developmental specialist and a physical therapist to ensure I meet my maximum potential in growth and development It is still early so I may see little effects from the scarring. I know God is able and the leader of my team. My mom and dad continue to let the doctors and nurses know that we believe in the power of prayer and that God will bring me to healing and wholeness and has placed each of them over my care to ensure my vision will come to be. Keep those prayers coming… whatever we need, thank God we can ask for it in the name of Jesus!

James 1:2-4
"Consider it pure joy, my brothers, whenever you face trials of many kinds, because you know that the testing of your faith develops perseverance. Perseverance must finish its work so that you may be mature and complete, not lacking anything."

Today was another quiet day. I have finally gained one whole pound since birth. I am now 2 lbs 5 oz. Kenya held me this morning and Mom held me this afternoon. The nurses did my care today (temperature, diaper changes, etc). I got another bath and looked very nice and smelled great when Mom, Dad and Kenya came to see me this evening.

While Mom was holding me, the nurse changed out my bedding. When she dressed me, she put me in an animal print outfit, my bedding all had animal print and the covering for my Isolete even had animals on it. When Mom got there she said it looked like Noah's Ark had arrived at the NICU, especially since it was a really rainy day today.

Mom and Dad received some tips from the physical therapist during my session today on different things they can do to get me ready to start drinking from a bottle or from my mom. Hopefully in the next couple of weeks, I will get to move to start drinking from a bottle!

Genesis 7:1
The LORD then said to **Noah**, "Go into the ark, you and your whole family, because I have found you righteous in this generation.

This morning I had alone time with Mom. It was really cool as she sang our special family "Good Morning" song. She almost always sings it to me each morning! The nurses had just started my feeding so I was snuggled in my bed eating when she arrived.

This evening I had alone time with Dad. He took my temperature and changed my diaper. He wrapped me up like a burrito to be sure I stayed warm before holding me for over an hour.

I weighed 2 lbs 5.6 oz tonight and really enjoyed my alone time with both Mom and Dad.

Today I was pooped. I didn't do much talking or looking around, I just spent a lot of time resting.

But one thing that I still did was keep the milk flowing right on through! The doctors increased my feedings to 20 mL every three hours and Mom, Dad and the nurses have a running joke about how regular I am as a result of the steady increases in my feeding amounts. Almost every time someone changes my diaper, I have filled it up, I'm in the process of filling it up, or as soon as I have a fresh diaper on, I fill that fresh diaper up! So today, I was pooped — literally and figuratively.

For all of you who want to know what Mom and Dad will need when I come home... lots and lots of diapers!

Also, today I weighed 2 lbs 6.4 oz and Dad did my temperature and changed my diaper (yes, the daily present that Dad has come to expect was there waiting for him!) He held me and Mom and Kenya even stopped by for a late night visit after Kenya was done with her dance practice. As pooped as I was, I still opened my eyes to see my family.

DAY 50
BOYS NIGHT OUT

June 16, 2012

Mom came and saw me again this morning. She got a chance to hold me before it was time to go. It always feels good when Mom holds me in her arms!

Today, the doctors increased my feedings to 21 mL every three hours. Tonight, Mom took Kenya to her Dance Recital, so Dad came to see me for a Boys Night Out. Dad took my temperature, changed my diaper and held me for a whole two hours and it was great! We talked about all sorts of boy stuff and got a chance to bond.

Kenya was pooped from her Dance Recital last night, so Mom let her sleep in this morning and Dad had yard work to take care of, so Mom came and saw me by herself this morning.

Because Kenya had two more performances today, Mom, Dad and Kenya came and saw me early, in between Kenya's two performances. It was great that they came and saw me earlier because I was awake almost the entire time to see them. Kenya took my temperature, Dad changed my diaper and Kenya held me. It felt great to be back in my sister's arms!

Happy Father's Day!

I am still getting bigger and stronger on this road to full recovery. I weighed 2 lbs 8.4 oz today and had time with both Mom and Dad holding me. Kenya is back to visiting me in the evenings and taking my temperature.

I am thankful that I have a team of nurses and doctors that pay attention to all of my good days and my bad ones. My mom and dad always stay there and make sure that I am okay on bad days (which I don't have many of anymore). Often I have things going on internally that you can't see and since I can't talk and haven't started the loud, long cries, the only way the staff knows when something is going on internally is through the alarms. If my head isn't healing appropriately then there are scans to monitor that. It is often easy for the team to help me and monitor the physical growth and deficiencies but the internal challenges that I sometimes face can't be known without my alarms. People bigger than me can let you know something just isn't right by crying, screaming, making facial expressions or asking for help. If they can talk they may get silent and may isolate themselves and you know that something is wrong and you help them through it; you do not ignore it. Since I can't do those things, the doctors, nurses and my family listen to my alarms and respond to me consistently. They continue to always be there for me, never leaving my side when I alarm and standing by me until I recover. They encourage me to continue to gain weight and to breathe and, most importantly, they celebrate all of my milestones and when I am at 100% with breathing.

The road to recovery isn't easy and I know that many people are praying for me and God has placed many people in my life. It is truly wonderful to have people here monitoring my internal and external strength to ensure that I am strong inside and out and when I am not, they continue to be there for me and never leave me to struggle through it all alone!

Luke 10:32-34

"So too, a Levite, when he came to the place and saw him, passed by on the other side. But a Samaritan, as he traveled, came where the man was; and when he saw him, he took pity on him. He went to him and bandaged his wounds, pouring on oil and wine. Then he put the man on his own donkey, took him to an inn and took care of him."

On Friday, I turned seven weeks old. If I was still in my mommy's tummy she would be 32 weeks into the pregnancy. Next Wednesday, I will officially be two months old. So, we are following a lot of numbers but they are all very important.

Today was bath day *and* Mom, Dad and even Kenya got to hold me today. I felt the love from all angles. Kenya took my temperature and Mom changed my diaper.

As I continue to get older, the doctors are looking for me to be able to meet several milestones like eating from a bottle. I get to try drinking from a bottle for the first time next week. So far, I have been doing well with the pacifier but I do get tired after a few minutes and spit it out.

I will also have to graduate from my isolette and move into an open bed. This will require me to be able to maintain my temperature outside of my temperature controlled isolette. Lastly, my lungs will have to get a little bit stronger. Right now, I receive about three liters of oxygen flow through my nasal cannula; I will need to receive less support from the nasal cannula before I can go home. They are okay sending me home on oxygen but it will need to be minimal. The good news is that I do not have to be a certain weight which means I may be still a small guy when I go home. Once I'm home I may not be ready to be passed around for just a little while until I get stronger and my lungs and immune system get stronger.

Overall, today was a good day and we are just following the numbers; counting down the days until I get to go home!

That is what my doctor referred to me as today, "Small, but Mighty!"
Do you remember I told you that my head ultrasound from last week showed
scarring on my brain that could pose some long term challenges for me? I had
a follow-up ultrasound yesterday and this morning the doctors told Mom that
when they reviewed the ultrasound they did *not* see the scarring any longer!
God is truly awesome; no matter what the doctors' say, He is the ultimate
provider, restorer and healer! We didn't even know it was possible for this to
be reversed but as stated in Matthew 19:26 — Jesus looked at them and said,
"With man this is impossible, but with God all things are possible."

Not only is the scarring not showing, but the ventricles, which they
thought would possibly fill with fluid from the bleeding, are getting smaller.
If they weren't it would cause me to have a reservoir (a small temporary
access point inserted in my head to draw fluid out periodically) or a shunt
(a tube placed permanently in my head to keep the fluid draining that would
have prevented me from playing contact sports.) It is looking more likely
that I will not need the temporary reservoir inserted or the permanent shunt!

Also, today I weighed 2 lbs 11 oz. I have finally doubled my birth weight.
I am 14 inches long (I was 12.5 inches long at birth). The doctors increased
my feedings to 23 mL every three hours. I had no alarms today and had a
great time playing with Kenya. Dad took my temperature and changed my
diaper and Mom held me today.

Tomorrow, they are going to have me going back to lying on my mom's
chest to see if I search for feedings from her to get me prepared for bottle
feedings and, ultimately, nursing from Mom. Each day I get stronger and
stronger and God continues to show that although I am small he can still use
me to show just how Mighty he is!

Psalms 30:2
"O LORD my God, I called to you for help and you healed me."

I weighed 2 lbs 11.8 oz today and got to nuzzle up to Mom today and begin practicing nursing. I did a great job and turned my head back to try again every time Mom repositioned me.

Kenya took my temperature and Dad changed my diaper (he had to do it three times back to back because I kept going right when he would put a new diaper on or wipe me) and he also got to hold me for a little while. I have graduated from the micro-preemie diapers (who knew these even existed) to the preemie diapers which are a little big for me. The micro-preemie diapers weren't containing the contents so they had to move me to the next size.

Day 56
"Cooking for Clayton"

June 22, 2012

Today, Mom and Dad got the best news. As many of you know my mom does Pampered Chef. Ms. Sherri Gaster who recruited Mom put on a "Cooking for Clayton" fundraiser just for me! Grandma was there with a few of her friends and Aunt Tracy and Uncle Demario helped pull it all together and mail the donation to me. Aunt Nikki and Aunt Tasha helped Aunt Tracy share the good news and surprise Mom, Dad and Kenya with all of the great details. Thank you to everyone for your continued love and support and a special thank you to all that contributed to and organized the fundraiser for me.

Today, I was 2 lbs 12 oz and Mom held me again for nuzzling and Kenya held me as well.

I want to leave you with the message that Aunt Tracy and Ms. Sherri shared with Mom and Dad that truly mirrors a lot of my experiences:

The Smell of Rain: http://www.2jesus.org/inspstories/rain.html

Today, I started the day nuzzling with Mom again; this time I was pretty tired and didn't do much responding to the test run of nursing. The doctors have decided that I am clinically stable with my head and that they are going to now move my head ultrasounds to every other week which is great! They are also going to try to wean me down a little on my nasal cannula from 3.0 liters of oxygen support down to 2.5 liters to see how I respond. The goal is still to get me down to 0.5 liters of oxygen before I go home.

Also, I am going to be in a research study which is exciting because Mom helps manage clinical trials for work. I will get to have massages (if I am in the treatment group and not the placebo group) three times a day to see if this helps with my growth, development and building my immune system. The study will go on for three months so I will let you know how things go! I am so excited to be so little and already getting massages. Mom was pretty jealous!

Today, Dad got me out of my bed for Kenya to hold me again. I weighed 2 lbs 13 oz; only 3 oz away from 3 lbs! I ended the day falling asleep with Kenya and Dad falling asleep with me.

DAY 58
SECOND CHANCES

June 23, 2012

As promised, the nurse asked the doctor if I could begin trying to wean down from 3 liters to 2.5 liters of oxygen through my nasal cannula again since it had been a week since I last tried. I did great and had no alarms this time.

Kenya had to take my temperature twice because it seemed a little low the first time but the second time it was good. I weighed 2 lbs 13.8 oz. Dad changed my diaper and I did nuzzling time with Mom twice. This morning I was too tired and fussy (yes, I really cried for a while) so Dad held me and made me feel much better and I calmed right down. This afternoon Mom let me try again at nuzzling and I did better.

Today was a great day of second chances and I did great!

Day 59
Pound for Pound

Good news! Today I hit 3lbs. I am getting to be such a big boy. I am at 24 mL feedings every three hours.

Tonight was bath night and Kenya gave me my bath and took my temperature. She was so excited and I didn't even cry or grunt while she was doing either.

Mom held me this morning to continue getting me to practice nursing and Dad held me this evening. It was a really quiet day today, so we just celebrated my growth.

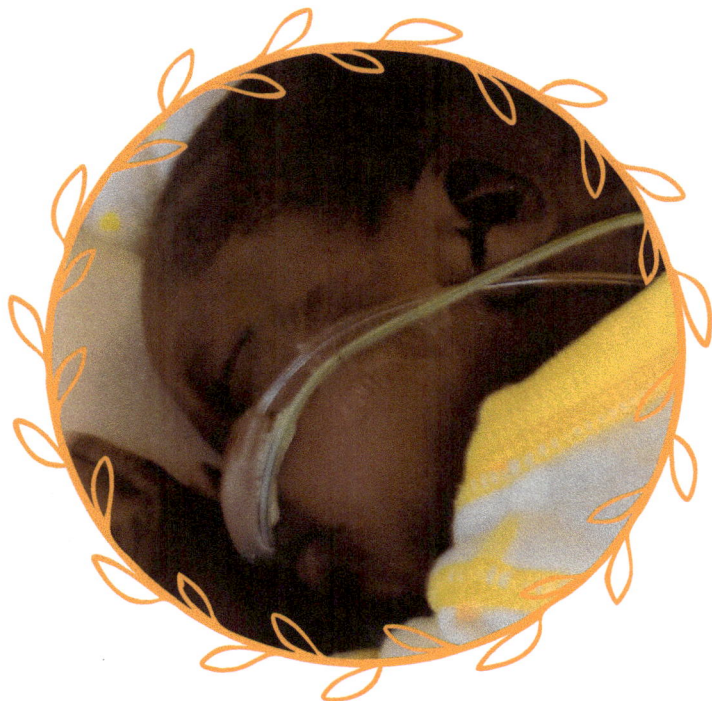

Still making improvements. Today my nurse took me off of pump feeding. My feeding tube was hooked up to a pump that released over a 30 minute period. Well, I am now at 26 mL every three hours and I still use my tube but it just hangs in my bed and gravity releases the milk into my tube; instead of taking thirty minutes, it all goes in within about five minutes or less.

Kenya was at Vacation Bible School (VBS) tonight and slept in this morning so I nuzzled with Mom this morning and cuddled with Dad this evening. Mom took my temperature and changed my diaper. When the nurse weighed me this evening, I weighed 3 lbs 0.8 oz.

The nurse hopes that in the next couple of weeks I will be moving from my Isolete to an open crib because I am getting to be so big and doing well maintaining my temperature when I am outside of my Isolete. I just need to be able to drink from a bottle and so far I am progressing well with sucking on my pacifier and testing out nursing from Mom. I actually got some milk in my mouth today which was weird, but I can't' resist and keep trying at it again and again.

Today was my first day as an enrolled participant in the massage study. Mom and Dad had training this evening. After Mom took my temperature, gave me a bath and changed my diaper, I received my first massage from her. I did so well! Before she starts each massage, the instructor told her she has to ask me for permission before starting the massage. I gave her permission tonight by looking right at her after she asked and I didn't cry, alarm or get the hiccups during the massage and that let Mom know that I was enjoying it.

Dad had to leave early to pick Kenya up from VBS at church tonight. She will not see me in the evenings again until Saturday when she completes VBS, but she did get up early with Mom this morning to come see me. We had a lot of fun too before Mom held me for more nuzzling practice.

I weigh 3 lbs 1.4 oz and had another eye exam today and will have another eye exam next week until my eyes mature further. Tomorrow the doctors are planning to reduce my oxygen levels down from 2.5 to 2.0 liter per minute because I am still doing so well. It was a busy day today and after my massage, the nurse began my feeding and I fell fast asleep!

June 27, 2012

I had a very special visitor. My grandmother came to visit me today. She will be staying with me for the weekend while my mom and dad are away at my Uncle Damon and my future Aunt Kimberly's wedding. So today things were a little different. I still got to nuzzle with Mom this morning and she gave me my morning massage. This afternoon, Grandma took my temperature, changed my diaper and held me. Dad gave me my evening massage and helped Grandma with me through each step.

The nurse today gave me the bottle for the first time. I was able to drink 5 mL of my 26 mL before getting tired and starting to alarm. It was very weird but very fun and I look forward to trying again. The doctors also weaned me down to 2.0 liters of oxygen today and I did great! I will be getting rid of the nasal cannula in no time if I keep up this good work.

LOVE

DAY 63
I AM COLD   *June 28, 2012*

It was a slow quiet day today. I didn't feel like doing much. The doctors increased my feeds to 28 mL every three hours. I am still growing very well and enjoyed seeing Mom, Dad, Kenya and Grandma today. I played with Mom this morning when I should have been nuzzling, but I will just try again tomorrow because I know how important it is to get in practice.

When Mom took my temperature it was a little lower than usual so they increased the temperature of my Isolete. Then when Grandma took it again this evening it was again a little low. I was supposed to get a bath tonight but they held off until I could warm up some.

Other than watching my temperature things were good today!

DAY 64
KEEP ON GROWING

June 30, 2012

Today was an active day. Mom and Dad came to see me before going to my Uncle Damon and new Aunt Kim's wedding in NY. Grandma and Kenya stayed behind to take care of me.

Dad gave me a massage before leaving and let me nuzzle one more time as well. Both Mom and Dad held me and it was great. I am going to miss them, but I am very excited to spend some time with Grandma and Kenya.

Grandma held me this afternoon and changed my diaper. Kenya took my temperature and teased me with the pacifier to keep me smiling.

I weighed 3 lbs 5 oz today and had a good day.

DAY 65
MOVING ON "DOWN"

I am now down to 1.5 liters of oxygen going through my nasal cannula. I did very well on my first day at this level. Mom and Dad called to check on me this morning and this evening.

Grandma and Kenya did my care today and held me again. The nurse also gave me a bath this evening. I weigh 3 lbs 6 oz. It is great that my weight continues to go up and I am breathing better so oxygen levels keep moving down.

The doctors are still giving me a dose of caffeine to help with my lung development, but they are thinking of taking me off of it at 34 weeks which is what I would be on Monday if I was still in my mom's tummy. We are getting even closer to the possibility of me going home without a nasal cannula!

I am so excited today because Mom and Dad were back to see me after being out of town. I was on my best behavior for them. When Grandma came to see me this morning, I continued to rest and wouldn't open my eyes so that I could save all my energy for Mom and Dad. The nurses told Mom and Dad that I had three alarms; one yesterday, one overnight and one this morning, each occurring about thirty minutes after eating.

Dad took my temperature, changed my diaper and gave me my massage which usually puts me to sleep. Today's visit was different, I was awake the entire time Mom and Dad where there for an hour and a half. It was the longest I had ever stayed awake with them and it was so much fun. Dad showered me with lots of kisses; Mom held me and let me have some nuzzling time.

My feedings were increased to 29 mL every three hours and the doctors and nurses continue to say that they are so happy with how well I am doing. But I am just glad that Mom and Dad are back!

DAY 67
TASTE AND SEE   *July 2, 2012*

More new experiences that continue to show that I am growing. Today, I drank from a bottle for the first time. I drank 15 mL ($^1/_2$ an ounce) of milk this afternoon and then drank another 7 mL this evening. Of course, I got tired both times, so they finished my feeding through my feeding tube both times. But, boy the taste was so good; it was cool to see them get my bottle and I immediately searched for it and started to drink from it when they put it to my mouth. The nurses, doctor and Mom and Dad were very proud of me.

I now weigh 3 lbs 8.8 oz. Dad gave me a bath today. Mom gave me a massage this morning and Dad gave me a massage this evening. I love drinking milk from a bottle — it tastes great!

Psalms 34:8
"Taste and see that the Lord is good; blessed is the one who takes refuge in him."

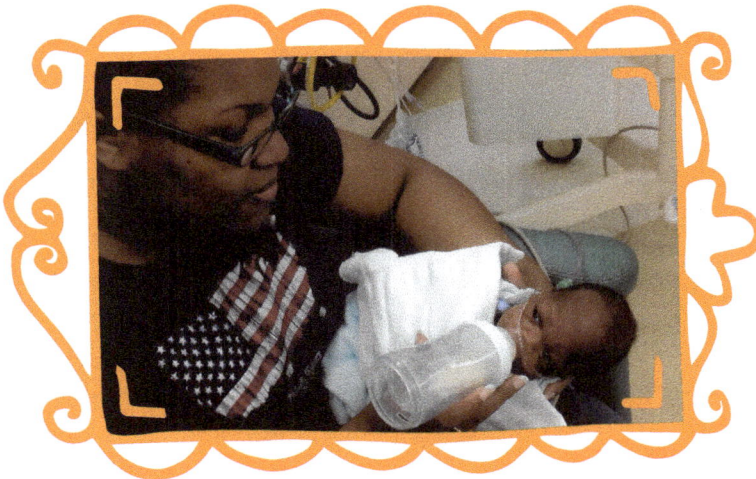

Today, I took 20 mL of my 29 mL feeding this morning. We were so excited. The doctors also increased my feedings to 30 mL (1 ounce). I also weigh 3 lb 9 oz. Grandma and Mom held me this morning and Kenya held me this evening and took my temperature. Mom gave me my morning massage and Dad gave me my evening massage and changed my diaper.

The doctors talked to Mom and Dad this evening about how they felt there was nothing to explain how well I am doing and how I have overcome each of the obstacles that were in front of me. The doctors attribute it to Mom and Dad coming every day to see me, talking to me, holding me and encouraging me to continue to do my best. Mom and Dad thanked the doctors for all that they have done for my growth and development. Mom and Dad also reminded them that they truly believe that there is nothing God can't do and that He worked through my doctors and nurses to help me get to this point and overcome these obstacles.

It is great to be a living witness of how great God is and I am glad that opportunities like these continue to allow Mom and Dad to share this with others!

DAY 69
INDEPENDENCE DAY
July 4, 2012

Today was another day of continued growth and strides towards independence for me.

When Mom and Grandma came to visit this morning, they were greeted with a picture of me holding an empty bottle from last night! That's right, I started my Independence Day by drinking an entire feeding from the bottle!

Mom, Dad, Kenya and Grandma came to visit me tonight. Dad took my temperature, changed my diaper, gave me a bath, helped weigh me and gave me my evening massage. I weighed in tonight at 3 lbs 10 oz and my feedings were increased to 31 mL every three hours.

I also received the results from my eye exam and they show continuous improvement to my vision!

It feels good to continue moving towards my independence.

DAY 70
BOTTLES UP

Well, you are going to be so proud of me. I drank an entire bottle during the night and this morning for Mom, then again at 11 a.m. I was tired for my next two feedings. For my evening feeding I was a little tired and nursed a little from Mom and then took almost my entire bottle except 6mL.

I also was able to move down to 1.0 Liter of oxygen support from 1.5 Liters and by the end of the night I hadn't had any alarms.

Grandma changed my diaper once this morning and this evening after I ate. Kenya took my temperature, changed my diaper with Dad coaching her along the way and put my new outfit on for the night just before Mom nursed. I weighed 3lbs 13oz and am 15 inches long. My weight has finally caught up to Kenya's birth weight and the doctors and nurses have moved their guesses for when I will go home to before August... yay!

DAY 71
THE LITTLE ENGINE THAT COULD   *July 6, 2012*

I am continuing to practice drinking from the bottle while trying to remember to breathe. More importantly, I have to remember to stay awake also while I eat. That seems to be the biggest challenge. Who knew eating could be so hard! I have eight feedings in 24 hours. I am usually able to take half of those from the bottle and the rest of the time, I am usually tired and have to take my feeding from my feeding tube.

Today was bath night again, and Dad gave me a bath and then gave me my bottle. Kenya took my temperature and changed my diaper this evening. Grandma took my temperature and changed my diaper this morning while Mom gave me my bottle. I have finally been doing a good job of burping, sometimes without even needing a pat on the back.

For now the plan is for me to continue to get better at taking my bottle while remembering to breathe and, of course, continuing to grow! The only difference between me and the train in "The Little Engine That Could" is that I have never doubted myself and know that God has me in the palm of his hands!

DAY 72
FAMILY TIME

July 7, 2012

Today was another day of steady progress and good news for me. This morning, Mom, Dad and Grandma came by. Grandma took my temperature and changed my diaper and Mom cuddled with me and gave me my morning feeding. My doctors told me this morning that I may have my last head ultrasound at the NICU soon because I am doing so well that I may not be here for too much longer!

This evening, I spent more time with Mom, Dad and Grandma and I got a chance to spend more time with my sister. Kenya took my temperature and changed my diaper (she's getting really good at it). Mom and I nuzzled again and Mom fed me again from the bottle and I drank the whole thing!

I really like spending time with my family!

DAY 73
BLESSED AND HIGHLY FAVORED

July 8, 2012

Today was another good day. Grandma and Mom came to see me this morning before leaving to go to North Carolina. Grandma will be back to visit when I go home and Mom will be back bright and early to see me on Wednesday.

Grandma did my temperature and diaper one final time to conclude her trip and Mom held me and fed me again this morning. They both gave me lots of hugs and kisses before leaving.

Dad and Kenya finished the day with me. Kenya took my temperature. Dad changed my diaper, held and fed me tonight. I have been drinking from a bottle for every feeding and taking it all like a big boy should. I may be moving on to the next step tomorrow because I am doing so well. The nurse hopes to remove my feeding tube and move me to an open bed tomorrow. My milk is also no longer getting the extra calories put in it as of today because I am getting so big from Mom's milk.

I weigh 3 lbs 14 oz and am so excited to know that with each new experience I continue to receive God's blessing and am living a highly favored life!

Well, so much good news to report today. Dad came to visit me this morning and was greeted with some nice surprises. First, he was happy to see that my feeding tube had been removed. I am now doing all feedings by bottle. Second, I am now in an open bed, so no more temperature controlled bubble.

After Dad fed me breakfast and held me for a while, we got the most exciting news! The doctors are ready to let me go home with Mom, Dad, Kenya and our dog Felipe. If all continues to go well, the doctors plan to let me go home as early as next Tuesday! They also lowered my oxygen support down to 0.5 liters from 1.0 liters. That is just one step away from having my nasal cannula removed.

Also, I hit the big 4.0 (that is pounds) today! This means that I will get my first round of immunizations soon. After Kenya took my temperature and changed my diaper, she fed me dinner and held me until I fell fast asleep. It was a very exciting day for everyone and I am so excited to learn that I get to finally come home soon to meet so many of you.

Yesterday, I shared that my feeding tube was removed and I was moved to an open bed because I was progressing so quickly. Well today, I decided that I liked the cozy comforts of my Isolete better than the open bed, so I made enough noise until the nurses decided to move me back to my climate controlled palace!

Dad came to see me this morning. We had a great conversation while he fed me breakfast. We talked about the plans that the Lord has for me and how they are plans to see me prosper and not to fail. He was also telling me that he is very proud of me for all the strength and courage that I am showing while I continue to grow.

This evening, Dad came back and we spent some more time talking and laughing. Dad took my temperature, changed my diaper and fed me half of my dinner because he had to pick up Kenya from church (she is a member of the Zion's Praise Dance Ministry and they rock)!

I'm looking forward to seeing Mom tomorrow after she returns. I have so much to tell her and so much love to show!

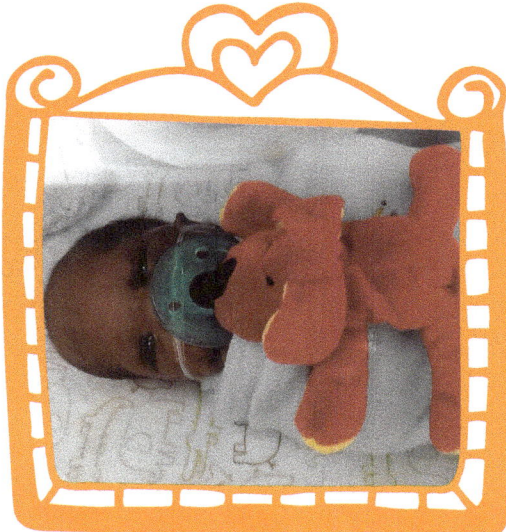

Today was much better! I only had one alarm today. The doctors have decided to hold off on my immunizations and give me some time to focus on getting through my feedings with less spitting up. They have added rice cereal to my milk and they have to do some special cutting of the nipple to allow it to flow at just the right speed.

Mom came back and was there to see me bright and early this morning with Dad. When she saw all the cutting they had to do to get my flow right, the nurse told Mom that she could buy nipples that would have the Y-cut needed. Mom came back to see me just before lunch time and brought me my own nipples and bottle for me to use for the rest of my stay here.

When Mom, Kenya and Dad came back to see me tonight, the nurse had already given me a bath, took my temperature and weighed me. I now weigh 4 lbs 1 oz and am 16 inches long! That fancy new bottle set-up Mom gave me worked like a charm as I had very little spit-up with these so the nurses were very excited about that (and so were Mom and Dad). Throughout the final transitions of coming into this world, my stay in the NICU and going home, I continue to find the strength within and know that when Mom, Dad, the nurses and doctors have done their part, God will be my continuous help!

Psalm 121: 1-3, 5-8
"I lift up my eyes to the mountains — where does my help come from? My help comes from the Lord, the Maker of heaven and earth. He will not let your foot slip — he who watches over you will not slumber;... The Lord watches over you — the Lord is your shade at your right hand; the sun will not harm you by day, nor the moon by night. The Lord will keep you from ALL harm — he will watch over your life; the Lord will watch over your coming and going both now and forevermore.

DAY 77
STICKING TO THE ROUTINE

July 12, 2012

Today was a normal routine day. Mom came to visit this morning and took my temperature, changed my diaper, fed me and gave me my morning massage.

This afternoon, Mom, Dad and Kenya came by and Dad fed me then Kenya held me. There were no changes in my care however; I did surprise everyone by eating 45 mL of milk tonight with one and a half teaspoons of cereal mixed in. This is up from 35mL at my last feeding. My spitting up is improving except I don't like my multivitamins with iron that much. I still try to spit that out.

Other than that, today was just a day for me to continue to rest and get stronger to be ready to go home soon.

Boy, today was rough. I did well this morning with Mom, but this evening not so good. When Mom, Dad and Kenya came to visit me, I just tuckered out and every alarm that could go off did. After the nurse got me back in my bed and helped me with my breathing, I had to get my feeding tube put back in. I just had no energy to do anything.

So, just a week ago I was almost walking out the door, but now I need to step back and slow down and get a few things under my belt. So, for now I will not be going home next week. The doctors said we will continue to take things one step at a time.

DAY 79
BACK ON TRACK

July 15, 2012

I am good! This morning when Mom and Dad came to visit, I was awake and happy. I took my entire bottle and stayed awake for a long time to talk to Mom and Dad. The nurses agree that going slow and steady is a much better approach for me.

I had my head ultrasound yesterday and things are still progressing nicely. I will not have to have another head ultrasound and will follow-up with the neurosurgeon shortly after I go home to be sure things still look good.

I also had a chest echo yesterday and things continue to look good. The only change is that the doctors are still trying to work through my possible reflux.

When Mom, Dad and Kenya came to see me tonight, the nurse had already taken my temperature, changed my diaper and weighed me. I am now 4 lbs 5 oz! Mom fed me (and I didn't, alarm or spit up) and Kenya held me after I ate. Dad gave me my morning and evening massage. The doctors also started me on Prevacid for my reflux. So far I am doing better. Finally, you remember I told you they had to put my feeding tube back in yesterday? Well, I didn't use it anymore after that one time, so I yanked it right out this afternoon to be sure the nurses knew that I didn't want it. They got the message… and now it is gone!

This morning, Dad came to see me. He fed me and I ate my entire 45 mL of milk with rice cereal and didn't have any alarms. The doctors and nurses told Dad that I will get another chance to come out of my Isolete again tomorrow and into an open crib.

This afternoon Mom, Dad and Kenya came to see me. Mom gave me a bath and fed me tonight. I again had no alarms and have been on the upswing for the last couple of days. I weighed 4 lbs 8 oz. I am just getting bigger and bigger every day!

DAY 81
THERE'S NO PLACE LIKE HOME

July 16, 2012

The nurses have instructed Mom and Dad to keep telling me that it is okay to come home. Every time I get really close, I end up alarming which signals that my heart rate is decreasing and / or I am not breathing well. Sometimes, I am not breathing that much and turn blue! Today, I did that three times! This morning just before my feeding I had my first alarm, so that put the feeding tube back in my nose. *But*, I did manage to keep my temperature up and have made it back into an open bed… hopefully, this time I will stay out in the open.

The doctors said as soon as I get my act together and stop with the alarms, I will be out the door. I am doing well with everything else; just keep forgetting to breathe sometimes. But, since I am still a preemie this is expected. If I was still in Mom's tummy I would be just at 36 weeks. To be considered full term is to be greater than 38 weeks, so the nurses, Mom, Dad and Kenya have been very forgiving of my need to get a little bit of oxygen support every now and then.

Tonight, Kenya took my temperature and Dad changed my diaper and gave me a massage while Mom fed me. Kenya promised me that there is no place like home and that Mom and Dad have a special room just for me. She said that she is ready to have me at home and that she knows I can continue to be a big boy and remember to breathe because she doesn't like seeing the nurses having to help me breathe. I will keep trying to remember to breathe so that I can make my way home!

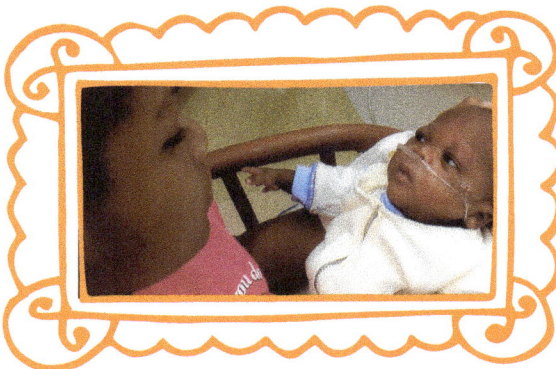

This body of mine is still growing. I had another alarm this morning while Mom and Dad were talking to the doctors about my next steps. The doctors were concerned and had me get a dye test to see if I was truly refluxing. The pediatric surgeon talked to Mom and Dad and said that I need surgery to close a small valve to no longer allow food to come back up after I eat it. If it is not fixed, I will be in a greater risk of SIDS (sudden infant death syndrome). While doing this surgery, the surgeon told Mom and Dad that they are also going to remove my appendix since they are already in there.

I am scheduled for surgery on Thursday and it will take seven to ten days for me to recover since I am so small and then I should be all set to go home. Just like clay, my body is still being molded so this surgery will allow me to fully develop into a strong structure. Right now, my structure has a little crack that needs to be filled.

I am now 4 lbs 10 oz and am still in my open bed doing great maintaining my temperature. Mom fed me this morning and Dad gave me a bath, took my temperature and changed my diaper tonight. Although, I am currently "Clay" ton under construction, I know that The Potter will gently mold and make me whole while still allowing my light to shine through the crack.

Jeremiah 18:3-4,6

So I went down to the potter's house, and I saw him working at the wheel. But the pot he was shaping from the clay was marred in his hands; so the potter formed it into another pot, shaping it as seemed best to him... "O house of Israel, can I not do with you as this potter does?" declares the Lord. "Like clay in the hand of the potter, so are you in my hand, O house of Israel."

Not much occurred today. The details of my surgery were confirmed with Mom and Dad. I am scheduled for surgery at 11 a.m. tomorrow.

Mom did all of my care this morning including my massage and feeding. Kenya took my temperature and changed my diaper this evening while Dad fed me. I now weigh 4 lbs 11 oz and am 16.5 inches long.

For all of you prayer warriors out there, be sure to send a special prayer up for me and the team that will be performing my surgery and handling my care. I know that God is in control and I look forward to giving everyone a good report tomorrow!

Day 84
It's the Final Countdown

July 19, 2012

I had my surgery today and there were no complications. Mom and Dad were there with me before, during and after the surgery. The surgeon even gave me a teddy bear surgeon that he signed and dated to help me remember this day. I am now resting and on the ventilator and tons of pain meds to keep me comfortable until I can get stronger.

I hope to be off my ventilator tomorrow. By the time Mom, Dad and Kenya came to see me this evening; I was peaking to see them. We are now in the final countdown until I can go home. As soon as I am able to return to breathing on my own and taking all my feedings by the bottle, I will be ready to go home. Because I am a preemie, my recovery may be a little slower but I am glad we are in the final stretch!

Nothing much new occurred today. Today the doctors focused on keeping me comfortable. I am still on the ventilator and the pain medication. When Mom, Dad and Kenya came to see me throughout the day, I was still pretty tired. I was opening my eyes a little bit but mostly just wanted to lay there and continue to get stronger.

The doctors are listening to see if my lungs sound clear and that my stomach is starting to make sounds. These would all be good signs that my body is waking up from all of the medicines given during the surgery. For now, the plan is to keep me comfortable and start to wean me off the pain medicine and the ventilator.

DAY 86
SLOW GOING

July 21, 2012

Today was a little bit better. The nurses cleaned me up with a small bath. My stomach is making sounds and my body is starting to have more activity.

The doctor tried to remove my ventilator today but I was not ready; I started off strong and then got tired so they had to put it back in. By the time Mom, Dad and Kenya came to see me this evening I was much more alert. Kenya held my hand to be sure I stayed comfortable.

Recovery for my little body is a slow process, but I am starting to feel better and get going in the right direction — which is out the door!

This morning I woke up pretty upset. First the nurse had to check my temperature, change my diaper and reposition me since I am still on the ventilator. Second, I am much more alert so I have realized just how much I do not like the ventilator. I tried to pull it out but Mom and the nurse were just too quick and were much stronger than me and were able to pull my hands off the tube. Third, I am hungry; these people still will not feed me yet. All of these things just really put me in a bad mood this morning. Mom got to hold me this morning and that helped to get me to calm down because I hadn't been in anyone's arms since my surgery on Thursday.

When the doctor came to see me this morning, she said that my blood levels were low due to the frequency of blood work I am getting and I would need some blood, so this afternoon I was given some blood to try to bring my levels up. She also decreased my oxygen rate to allow me to work at breathing more on my own. Plus, she saw how fussy I was, so now I am getting 5 mL of milk every 3 hours to get me eating again.

Mom, Dad and Kenya came to see me this afternoon and this evening. Kenya checked my temperature and Dad changed my diaper and held me this evening. When the doctor came back by to see me, she saw that I was awake and breathing much better so they are going to take me off the ventilator tomorrow and I am praying this time it is gone for good. I am ready to get back to my full feeds and drink my milk from the bottle!

I spent my day huffing and puffing. The doctor took me off the ventilator again today; I didn't do too well at first. My throat is really swollen so I was having a very hard time breathing. The doctor tried to put me back on the ventilator for a third time since the surgery but my throat was just too swollen to get the tube back in. So, the doctor moved me back to the CPAP at a rate of 10 liters. Just as the doctors put me on the CPAP, Mom and Dad came to visit.

I was pretty upset and the nurse had Mom and Dad try and help me calm down. Dad knew just what to do; he held my head and my feet which made me feel really good! By the afternoon, I was a little calmer except when the nurses messed with me. When Mom and Dad came to see me this afternoon, I was really frustrated. They had to hold me down again to keep me calm. The nurse then spoke with the doctor who agreed to move me from the CPAP mask back to the nasal cannula which I was on before my surgery. They started me at six liters and the goal will be to get me back down to ¾ liters. I am still on room air so my lungs are doing exactly what they are supposed to do. I just need my airway to open back up from the reflux and the aggravation of having the ventilator tubes down my throat.

The doctors have me on Prevacid for a week and steroids until tomorrow and I got a breathing treatment. I am now up to 10 mL every three hours through my feeding tube (now in my stomach) and they hope to move me back to a bottle tomorrow. Dad got to hold me tonight and I did very well and was so calm; it was the best to be back in his arms! I am looking forward to going back to my morning and evening holds tomorrow and getting back in my big boy crib!

DAY 89
WINDING DOWN

July 24, 2012

I met all of the goals the doctors set for me today! I am now on full bottle feedings at 25 mL and will be increasing to 35 mL every three hours late tonight. This is my minimum amount so another milestone accomplished. Since I have been back on the milk, I have only had Mom's milk. Tomorrow the doctors are going to add the extra calories to fortify my milk to be sure my bones grow nice and strong.

I did great on my nasal cannula and they now have me down to 1.5 liters in just a little over room air. I was still a little fussy all throughout the day but being able to eat more has definitely helped! I am still a little puffy from the fluids and all the air coming through my nasal cannula so the doctors gave me a dose of Lasix. That was the last medication I needed to receive through my IV so they are going to take that out later tonight as well. I was so puffy tonight that I weighed in at over 5 lbs!

The doctors are thinking of giving me my immunizations in the next couple of days, so my time is finally winding down in the NICU!

Moving forward the doctors will be making minor adjustments to my air supply through my nasal cannula. Right now the thinking is that I will go home on a little air support with my nasal cannula. Also, (keep praying that this time it holds) the doctors are planning for me to go home on Tuesday, July 31st just in time to celebrate Kenya's birthday the next day. I will get my two month shots this weekend.

As long as I do not have any alarms (I had one today) nothing should interfere with this discharge date. When I have a feeding alarm like I did today, I am not allowed to go home for six days from the date of the alarm. When I have a sleeping alarm, I am not allowed to go home for seven days from the date of the alarm. I am trusting God that there are no more alarms!

I am up to eating 45-50 mL at each feeding and my weight tonight was actually 5 lbs 3 oz and I am now 17 inches long. I was not as puffy today and my IV is gone! I am adjusting well to the minor changes the doctors make each day and I am so glad to have a new target date to be with Mom, Dad, Kenya and our dog Felipe.

Psalms 20:7
"Some trust in chariots and some in horses, but we trust in the name of the Lord our God."

DAY 91
THE HOME STRETCH

Today, the doctors took me back down to the settings I was on for my oxygen prior to my surgery. I am now on ¾ liters and 100% oxygen support; this is the level that allows me to go home. The doctors are going to try to continue to wean me down until I go home. I did great the entire time with my new flow.

Mom and Dad also completed choking and CPR training since I will be going home with oxygen and have a monitor. I am now up to drinking 2 ozs of milk (60 mL). I drink every drop of it and then for some reason I fall right to sleep as soon as I finish. I get my immunizations tomorrow; I also turn three months old tomorrow.

Tonight I weighed 5 lbs 4oz and am now back on my multivitamins with iron. We are in the *home stretch* and tomorrow Mom and Dad will get some more discharge instructions since now I will be going home on Wednesday. Kenya said it will be the best birthday present. She was able to find out that she was going to have a brother or sister for Christmas and now I am coming home to celebrate her birthday!

DAY 92
SHOTS

July 27, 2012

It was a busy day today. I received five vaccines today (given with two shots) in my legs. I also had my hearing test and passed. Later tonight, I have to pass a car seat test (sit in my car seat for three hours without alarming) to make sure I will be ok to ride in a car seat when it's time to go home.

The best part of my busy day is the doctors told Mom this morning that they are going to let me go home early! I go home on Monday now. They also reduced my oxygen down to 0.5 liters at 100%.

When Kenya and Mom came to see my tonight, Kenya changed my diaper and Mom gave me a bath. I am not a big fan of bath time, but no matter how much I cry they still give me one. I am now weighing 5 lbs 6 oz. After I pass the car seat test, I really will be finished with my assessments and can be ready to head out the door as long as I do not have any feeding or sleeping alarms between now and going home on Monday!

DAY 93
SITTING PRETTY

July 28, 2012

Last night I had my car seat test. I passed by sitting pretty and stayed quiet in my car seat from 11 p.m. — 2 a.m. (from one feeding to the next) without any alarms. So, I am looking forward to the road trip home. Today, Mom told the nurses that she feels like she has been a part of a Grey's Anatomy or ER series for the past three months as we have learned so many medical terms and so much about how my body works.

Kenya fed me this morning and when it was time for her, Mom and Dad to leave Dad picked me up from Kenya to put me back in my crib. I was not happy because Kenya and I were having so much fun. This evening, I took my feeding from Mom for the second time since my surgery and it was great. I went fast asleep during the feeding.

I now weigh 5 lbs 7 oz. Tomorrow, I have my final lab work at the hospital to be sure I am all clear to go home!

So, I hear there is this famous tell of the Night before Christmas however, I have a special story about the night before discharge. Many of the nurses and staff came by to talk to me, Mom, Dad and Kenya because it would be their last time seeing us since they were off tomorrow.

Mom and Dad were busy working with my lead nurse starting to pack up some of my things. The doctors ordered all of my final tests today to give my new doctors a starting point on what I have been through and how I was just before I left. I had labs drawn (they were beautiful) and an X-ray done as well. I had my going home photos taken. I was wide awake for my pictures and didn't cry!

Mom and Dad received another car seat from one of our church members and a stroller; so far they haven't had to purchase any of the larger items as our lovely church family has given me a crib, rocker, bouncer, swing, pack-n-play, bassinet, gift cards, clothes, a blanket and so much more! My room (and my *temporary* location in Mom and Dad's room for overnight) are all set up! I am so excited to see my home and my dog and meet everyone that I can soon!

Tomorrow will be another busy day, but tonight I got my last bath at the NICU by Dad. Kenya took my temperature then Mom fed me. I weighed in a little less today at 5 lbs 5.4 ozs, but check back in tomorrow for my final post from the NICU.

Wow... this morning was all tears of joy. Saying thank you to the people that cared for me over the last three months was very hard for Mom and Dad to do. It is truly amazing how far I have come, I have beaten the odds of having a permanent shunt in my head that would have limited my contact sports dreams and now still have a chance to live out my vision. I overcame severe lung disease that now has me on temporary oxygen support. I successfully underwent two major surgeries, one to repair a hole in my heart and another to eliminate acid reflux that threatened to take my life. Ain't God good! (Don't tell Mom and Dad that I didn't use proper English — but that is just how good God has been to me). This is just what we expressed to the staff to let them know that they did an incredible job providing medical care and allowing God to use them and sometimes step in for them when things went from the possible to the impossible. Kenya even gave the staff flowers (she made 100 of them!)

The ride home was really quick and my dog is so cool! He smelled me and stayed in my room most of the day. When I first got home, when I made any noise, everyone came in to see what I was doing (including Felipe). It is too easy here; the nurses didn't do that!

Tomorrow, I have an eye appointment and then go to meet my pediatrician on Wednesday. I also will get to meet my church family on Wednesday evening so I will have a lot to share on Sunday with you.

Thank you so much for all of your love, support and prayers. God has truly blessed me along this journey and I am so glad to be home, it is truly *sweet*!

Below is the scripture included in the flowers to the nurses as I know that the faith of my family that was bestowed unto me truly has healed me and allowed me to be a living testimony and a miracle for all to soon meet.

Matthew 17:20

Truly I tell you, if you have faith as small as a mustard seed, you can say to this mountain, 'Move from here to there', and it will move. Nothing will be impossible for you.

NOW WE GO HOME

In the days, weeks and months after documenting every day of Clayton's progress in the NICU, Clayton went on to face new challenges.

During the first week I was home it was very fun and interesting getting to know Mom, Dad, Kenya and Felipe. Being with them all day is completely different from seeing them twice a day.

I had a follow-up appointment with the eye doctor and they no longer need to see me until next year because my eyes are fine and I am not developing retinopathy of prematurity which can cause blindness. So, all clear with the eyes!

I also visited my pediatrician for the first time. She was super nice. I now weigh 5 lbs 10 oz. She said that I should be able to get off my oxygen support very soon. I am growing as expected and she said I look very good. I do not have to go back to see her for another month.

Lastly, I had an appointment to follow-up for my head. My head is where it is expected to be for growth but I have to have an ultrasound next month to see how things look. I will continue to follow-up with the neurologist for the next year and a half to ensure I am continuing to develop appropriately.

So far, things are good and I am working really hard with Mom and Dad to get on a sleep schedule but I am awake a lot during the day which is so much fun!

This second week was nice and quiet. We relaxed at home and spent time getting to know each other. I am eating between 2 — 2.5 oz every three hours and am waking up every three hours at night to eat. The doctor has added .5 oz of apple juice mixed with .5 oz of water to my diet to help me with digestion.

I had a follow-up appointment with the surgeon to see how I was healing from my stomach surgery. He said things look good and I should be able to have my g-tube removed in two weeks. I do not like to get that cleaned so I will be really glad to have it removed.

During Week Three, there was a big celebration for me. Some members from my church and my dad's job, as well as my grandma, celebrated having me at home. I received a lot of diapers, wipes, clothes and other items that I really needed. It was so much fun to see everyone and to learn just how much they care. *Thank you* to all that came and brought wonderful gifts for me.

I also had an appointment with my cardiologist. He was super impressed with how much I have grown and how well my heart looked. Everything seemed to be functioning well when they reviewed my ECG and ECHO (two tests to look at my heart and lung function because they go hand and hand). I have to go back to see him in two months.

When I turned four months old I began making small steps to get bigger. If I was born on time, I would really be just over two weeks old (this is my adjusted age).

Week Four was pretty busy. Mom had to interview with a development specialist to learn more about my current development. I have to go through an assessment with a physical therapist and a special instruction therapist (like an occupational therapist for adults) that will see how I am developing physically and mentally. If I am functioning at my adjusted age at the time of the assessments, I will be eligible for physical therapy and special instruction therapy through my insurance until I am three years old (or until my development catches up to my real age).

I also had my appointment to have my g-tube removed on my four month birthday! I was so glad to have it out, but now I have a big bandage covering the hole in my stomach. The surgeon said that spot should heal in just two to three days... which is amazing!

Then came Week Five at home; wow, what a week! This week, I had an appointment with the pulmonologist (lung doctor). I am finally finished with my Prevacid for my acid reflux, but I have still been having minor issues with refluxing. My breathing has been doing great so the nurse practitioner that I see said that my X-rays looked good and I sounded good when she listened to my lungs. She lowered my oxygen level from .5 liters to .25 liters. The monitor that I wear every day assesses how well I am breathing. She received a report from my monitor and called us after the appointment to let us know that I was doing so well that I can stop using the oxygen during the day and only wear it at night.

This news was perfect because we went out of town this weekend to visit my family in North Carolina. I met so many more people including a lot of my mom and dad's friends during a dinner that they had to meet me. Thank you to everyone that came to see me and provided me with more great gifts! I am so blessed and so thankful to be off this oxygen during the day.

Psalm 69:30
"I will praise God's name in song and glorify him with thanksgiving."

By Week Six, I only had one doctor appointment. When I visited my pediatrician this week, I weighed in at 7 lbs 7 oz and 19 inches long. I also received four vaccines during this visit. I wasn't too happy about that, but I didn't cry for very long.

I am now eating about 2.5 — 3 oz every three hours and Mom and Dad have been focusing on helping me continue to grow. Kenya helps watch me when she gets home from school but it doesn't last for very long because she has homework and dance class almost every day. Things are continuing to progress very well.

Week Seven was going well until that Friday. Overnight, I had a pretty bad reflux experience that caused me to not eat and not feel good at all. My temperature was a little low and I was pretty out of it. As soon as my pediatrician's office opened my mom took me in to be seen. I wasn't using the bathroom that much and Mom had put the monitor on me (I had just been approved to stop using the monitor continuously) to check my heart rate, respiratory rate and oxygen levels. The alarm went off twice noting that my respiratory rate and oxygen levels were periodically dropping.

This happened while I was in the doctor's office as well so they had me to go to the hospital for some extra tests. The doctor thought that maybe I had some of the fluids that I refluxed up go into my lungs or that I had RSV (a bad respiratory infection that can be very dangerous for a little guy like me). The doctor's admitted me into the hospital and did a chest X-ray, blood work and started an IV because I was pretty dehydrated by now since I hadn't eaten in a long time.

By late that evening, my chest X-ray came back normal, my blood levels were pretty okay, however, they had to repeat them because a few levels were a little low and the RSV test came back negative. I had finally started eating (only an ounce) at 12:30 p.m. (after not eating since 4 a.m.). I then drank two ounces at about 3 p.m. As soon as I finished that bottle I felt so much better. The doctors decided to keep me in for 24 hour observation. I was released the next day by noon. The doctors just think that the reflux episode caused my throat to have a little shock and zapped my energy causing me to be sluggish and not want to eat and have a little difficulty breathing.

Mom, Dad and Kenya took me home and as soon as I got there I was acting as if nothing had ever happened. It was quite a scare, but *thank God*, everything turned out to be okay. We all just decided that my body was having a little moment.

I Chronicles 16: 11-12
"Look to the Lord and his strength; seek his face always. Remember the wonders he has done, his miracles, and the judgments he pronounced,…"

Week Eight was another busy week. I had to follow-up with my pediatrician after going to the hospital. She put me back on my Prevacid except now I take a half tablet instead of a quarter of the tablet.

I also had my development evaluation this week. I had to do a lot of tests with the physical therapist and special instruction therapist. It took an hour and I was *very* tired. After it was all done I was showing skills that were equivalent to my adjusted age (which would be six weeks old) instead of the skills of an almost five month old. Because my skills are on target with my adjusted age they are not concerned, but because the goal is to have me developing on target with my real age I now have to begin physical therapy weekly and have special instruction every other week.

My last appointment was to have a head ultrasound. This appointment was to get updated images of the bleeding in my brain. The blood was still very visible so I received a copy of the ultrasound to take to my neurology appointment next week to be sure the bleeding has improved.

After being home for nine weeks, I had my neurology follow-up appointment. The neurologist did not have any concerns with my current progress and scheduled a follow-up appointment in five months. The neurosurgeon scheduled a follow-up appointment for two months from now and I have to have another head ultrasound. The images showed the bleeding looked pretty much the same but no improvement. He still isn't concerned but wants to continue to monitor it and hasn't ruled out if I will need a shunt placed in my head in the future. My weight at this appointment was 8 lbs 15 oz. We will keep praying that things get better.

I also started my special instruction this week. My therapist, Stacey, comes to visit me every other Friday morning at 8 a.m. Our primary focus right now is trying to get me to look and focus on objects with the ultimate goal in the next few weeks of tracking (following) objects. She said that black, red and white are my favorite colors and soft visual books are great to help me with this. Mom and dad went and picked me up some books and my Aunt Nikki and Uncle Darnell had already bought me a great mat with rings and toys that hang down from the polls attached to the mat. The mat is perfect for my therapy sessions because the toys are black and white!

By Week Ten, we still have another doctor's appointment. This week I visited the pulmonologist. She was happy with my current progress but with the winter months coming up she wanted to begin me on some medicines to help me, so that just in case I get sick, I would already have something to help me get over a cold and blunt the effects on my lungs.

So, get ready here are my new meds. I went from just taking a multivitamin and a half a tablet of Prevacid, to that plus:

     Albuterol inhaler — 2 puffs 12 hours apart daily

     Flovent inhaler — 2 puffs 12 hours apart daily

     Zantac oral — once daily one hour after I eat

This should help my lungs build up some defenses from getting sick.

I also went out of town to visit my Aunt Nikki, Uncle Darnell, Cousin Natalie and Grandma. We went down for a celebration for my new little cousin Emma that will be coming soon! Emma kept kicking me in her mom's tummy anytime her mom would hold me, but, my cousin showed me lots and lots of love. I don't know who hugged and kissed me more, her or Grandma!

By Week Eleven, we had new developments. This week, Dad was at home with me for a few days while Mom was out of town. We did some true male bonding. I also had my first physical therapy session. My therapist is Jessica. She has us working on my head control. She wants me to get tummy time and do exercises to strengthen my neck and midline. I also had another special instruction appointment with Stacey. We kept working on getting me to look at objects or people for a long period of time. This week, I have been hoarse and I had a very nasty cough (sounds like I have been smoking since I was born). The coughs last a long time and take my breath away.

Dad called the doctor's office on Friday and they had me come in immediately. When Mom and I got there the nurse practitioner listed to me and heard a little wheezing. My pediatrician also listened and they both decided it was time to take a trip back to the hospital for some additional testing.

When Mom and I arrived at the hospital they did a chest X-ray, blood work and a test for RSV. My chest X-ray and blood work came back normal. The test for RSV was negative but because the cough sounded so bad, the doctors at the hospital decided I needed to have a test for whooping cough. The test would take days to come back so they started me on the antibiotics for this as a precaution and decided to keep me for another 24 hours. I was released on Sunday and was instructed to take the full course of the antibiotics and they would call me for the results. If the test came back positive, the antibiotics would already be working to treat it.

By Week Twelve, I had a follow-up appointment with my pediatrician about my cough. My test for whooping cough came back negative. My cough has pretty much resolved but I still do not have my voice completely back. My pediatrician thinks that may be due to the reflux. I am not spitting up that often anymore so she thinks it may be internal and still aggravating my throat.

Other than that appointment, I have been continuing with my weekly physical therapy sessions and have started to show how strong I am. I fell asleep half way through my session this week but I did start to do a better job of holding my head up and have better neck support. So, I am feeling much better and am going back to making great progress.

Now, I have been home for thirteen weeks and, of course, I had a visit with the cardiologist. Everything looked good and he did another ECHO this time. He had no concerns about my first surgery to close the hole in my heart. I do not have to come back for three months for my next appointment.

I also had my first shot for my monthly Synergis which is a shot almost like the flu vaccine for adults except because I am a preemie, I have to get it monthly throughout the winter months. I didn't like this shot at all and kicked and screamed. They had to do the shot twice because the first time I kicked the needle out. I guess, since I weighed in at 10 lbs 1 oz at this appointment, they should have known I would be much stronger than the last time I had to get shots!

I am now 21 inches long and growing great. I met another little boy this week but he was only six weeks old but guess what... he was 10 lbs 15 oz and 23 inches long... that is too funny; because, I turned six months old this week and he is bigger than I am. But, just wait, I will catch-up with and surpass him in no time!

At Clayton's first birthday, we did a huge fundraiser and party for the March for Babies event that the March of Dimes in Central PA holds. He no longer receives his Synergis shots going into his second birthday and continues to wean off of his meds.

Clayton has gotten so big and with your support and prayers, as well as the advancement in medical care made possible in part by valuable research and funding by the March of Dimes, we are able to enjoy Clayton's many milestones and how he has surpassed many expectations.

In the years following his NICU stay, we continued to support the March of Dimes and support many family members and friends who also had preemies. Clayton has continued to grow by leaps and bounds. Now in North Carolina, Clayton is growing so fast and developing at an impressive rate. He completely feeds himself, tries to help us get him dressed and is now finally potty-trained at four years old. He walks with the assistance of a walker and will be walking short distances during the annual March of Dimes event. Clayton is Mr. Personality and we do hope that you have enjoyed his journey. Everyone shares the stories of wishing the baby will finally come and how painful it is, but I am so excited to share the other side of when you wished they would have stayed in just a little longer and the hope that there can still be a happy ending.

After all of this, I have my two kids, dog and a great home (not quite a ranch) and we are only missing the white picket fence; but, as you can see we will never say never on having that too one day. And, although Clayton still has mild challenges, he has been truly a blessing to our entire family and hope that his story has blessed you too!

ACRONYMS/GLOSSARY

Bilirubin	An orange-yellow substance made during the normal breakdown of red blood cells; passes through the liver and is eventually excreted out of the body; when elevated it can cause yellowing of the skin or whitening of the eyes (known as jaundice)
C-Section	Cesarean section
C-PAP	Continuous positive airway pressure
CPR	Cardio-pulmonary Resuscitation
ECG	Electrocardiogram (measures the rhythm of the heart over a period of time)
ECHO	Echocardiogram (cardiac ultrasound)
Isolete	An incubator for premature infants that provides controlled temperature and humidity and an oxygen supply
IUF	Intrauterine Fertilization
IV	Intravenous
Nasal Cannula	A device used to deliver supplemental oxygen or increased airflow to a patient or person in need of respiratory help
NICU	Neonatal Intensive Care Unit
Placebo	A harmless procedure prescribed more for the psychological benefit to the patient than for any physiological effect that is used as a control in testing new drugs or procedures
PICC	Peripherally inserted central catheter
STEM	Science, Technology, Engineering and Math

Banks Family

www.ingramcontent.com/pod-product-compliance
Lightning Source LLC
LaVergne TN
LVHW010314070426
835509LV00023B/3468